The Creator's Manual for Your Body

by
Dr. Jamie Fettig

Visit my websites at
www.Bazuji.com
www.TheCreatorsManual.com

Bauzji Publishing LLC.
Bazuji Inc

Bazuji Publishing LLC.
3854 53rd Street. S.E.
Tappen ND 58487

Cover Art Work by: Marcelline Harrisonfields©
For Original Prints and Details on Reproduction Rights, visit
www.Harrisonfields.com

ISBN 0-9761555-0-8

10 9 8 7 6 5 4 3 2 1

Thank You "I AM", the Creator.
For without you, none of this would be possible. None.

Also my mom, Monica Watkins. Thank you for who you are, who you have been for me, for everything you have done and for making all of this possible. The world and I owe most of this to you.

My sister and brother-in-law, Jolene and Joey Fettig. For always being there for me. For always believing in me and supporting me in what I do.

Extra Special Thank You to
My Dad - John Fettig
Jennifer Kleingartner
Diane LoMonaco
Kammie Gibbs
Amy Calvanese
Jolette Johnson
Melissa Smith - www.bodytalk.com.au

Special Thank You to
Mike Slusarchuck
Sharon Lawrence
Richard Kasvin
www.prints-posters.com
Mary Jurczyk
Lori Johnson
Grace Evans
Cindy Groves
Jessy LaPierre-Gonzalez
Katherine Ebacher

To everyone else whom I have encountered along the way, thank you.

The Life and Times of Dr. Jamie Fettig

I have been immersed in natural health ideas and concepts since before I was born. My mom never took me into the medical symptoms and disease care doctors. Growing up, the only time I saw a medical doctor was when I broke something or had to get a physical for school sports once a year. I pretty much ate whole fresh food my entire life. I never really got sugar, candy or junk food. I was always going outside and playing in the fresh air. We had symptoms and my mom just let our body heal itself. She never took us to the doctor for medications.

My dad went to a chiropractor when I was 5 years old because his back hurt and the chiropractor started talking to him about what chiropractic could do. The chiropractor talked about how the nerves in the body control everything: our moods, emotions, thoughts, immune system, digestion, healing, growth, muscles, intelligence, everything. Chiropractic makes sure the nerves are working better. My mom heard this message and started taking me and my two sisters to the chiropractor on a regular basis.

When I was 12 years old, I remember talking to one of my friends and asking him; You don't go to a chiropractor? Everyone goes to a chiropractor, what is wrong with you? What do you do when you get sick? He said, I go to the doctor. I said, but all they do is give you drugs to cover up your symptoms, they don't actually do anything to help you heal.

I went to a chiropractic college and was there to learn how to help people heal. So I read everything I could, and took every seminar I had money for, learning everything I could about health and well being. The Creator gifted me with an excellent mind, and I was able to remember most things I read, saw, and heard.

During college I spent some time in China working in a traditional Chinese hospital. I graduated from chiropractic college early and went straight into private practice. I used everything I knew that worked to help people in my practice heal and become well. Because of my knowledge I was able to help people heal from all different types of symptoms, diseases, and conditions.

This book is divinely inspired and designed to have you naturally wanting to be well. This book is based on my life experiences and what produced results for people in my life and people in my practice.

Disclaimer

This is not intended as a substitution for the
medical symptoms and disease care system.

This is intended to eliminate the need for the
medical symptoms and disease care system.

When you are healthy and well, there are no symptoms or
diseases left to treat. By the end of this book, you will know for
yourself that there are better ways to help your body heal than
the medical symptoms and disease care system or model.

Contents

Chapter 1

The Basics

I am writing this book because I know it will make a difference for you. It will give you what you want, make it easier to have the things you want, to enjoy life, have fun and to get everything that is important to you, whatever that is.

I have seen people's pain, fear, worry, and heartache. I have seen people go through needless suffering, people die needlessly from symptoms and disease that could have easily been helped. With this book, I intend to end that, for those who want this. I will bring you to a place of health and well being, with your permission, of course.

Health is easy; it is not meant to be complicated. Mother Nature has been at this for millions of years, and she knows what she is doing. We humans have screwed it up by thinking we could improve upon perfection.

A lot of what is woven into this book is taking you past your barriers, to actually be at a place where health is the natural expression and you don't even have to think about it. Much of this book is interwoven to allow you to see health as it really is, and to allow you to think accurately about health and well being, and how to get them both.

There is a big distinction I need to make right here. It is the difference between emergency medical care, and medical symptom and disease care. Emergency medical care is exactly that. It is the type of care you would get if you cut yourself, had an accident, slipped or fell, etc. Something happened, you are hurt, and you get medical care. Medical symptom and disease care is also exactly that. It is the part of medicine that deals with *trying*, and I emphasize trying, to help people heal their symptoms and disease.

Also, when I talk about the medical symptoms and disease care system, I am not talking about most doctors' intentions. Most doctors go into medicine because they want to help people. Most people sincerely want to do what is best for people. It is just that their entire training and way of thinking is all one-sided. Most of their textbooks and education is controlled and funded by people with financial interests in keeping traditional medicine in place. Mostly, it is not the individual people or their intent that is causing the harm. It is the ideas and one-sided thinking that they have accepted.

There will be times in this book when I ask you to "do" something, to think of something before you continue reading. **DO THIS!** You see, knowledge in and of itself might not do anything for you. You probably have done things before in the past, only to go back to your old ways in a couple months, or even weeks. These things I ask you to do are *simple* and powerful. You do not have to understand why you are doing them. They will work if you just do them. I urge you to get everything out of this book, for yourself, for your life, and for your family. Do NOT just go on reading without doing what the book is asking you to do.

I also teach with stories. They are not just warm fuzzy stories that you don't need to read. They are stories to help this book make the difference I promise it will make for you. Everything that is in this book is in here for a reason. So I encourage you to read everything in this book.

Much of what I will say will probably be directly opposite of what you already know, and what you think you already know, about health and well being. And yet, it will make so much sense, will feel so real to you, and you will hear for yourself how incredibly simple health and well being actually are. So sit back, relax, because by the end of this book you will be able to prove to yourself how even though much of this goes against what you already know, it will get you what you want: being healthy and well.

Stay out of the pitfall of tossing this aside or overly questioning it just because it is new. See, there is this interesting thing that happens with almost all humans. When something new comes along, no matter how much sense it makes, we often question it and discredit it because it is new. But no matter how mysterious or completely misunderstood something is, if it has seemingly been there forever, no one questions it. They just accept it. Like, when you eat food, how do you digest it? How does gravity pull things towards the earth? How do painkillers get rid of pain? Does the medical symptoms and disease care system actually help people heal? Whether or not what I am sharing with you is right or wrong is not the question. The question is, will it work for you? Will it give you the results you want? And if you do what is in this book, yes, it will.

Results and health are more than just having knowledge. Let's face it, if health were just about knowledge, we would all be healthy, because there is more information out there about health than there ever has been before. There is one little problem with all the knowledge out there. It is the limited and flawed intellect that keeps getting in the way, getting in the way of your inner knowing, your inner wisdom.

With all the diet plan books, health clubs, unused health club memberships, exercise books, exercise fads, and everything else available about the health and fitness industry, whom do you trust? How do you know who is providing you with the value you are looking for? Who can actually give you the happiness and security you are looking for?

How can any one book make or say anything different than anything that is already out there?

You may have spent hundreds of dollars on unused gym memberships, and made New Year's resolutions only to forget they even existed one month later. Have you gone on diet after diet without making any difference? Tried this exercise program or that one, maybe even hired a personal trainer, to no avail? Or maybe you found some complicated diet plan, and it took way too much time to keep it in your life.

This book is not any of that. This is about your life, your happiness, your family. This is about staying young, and looking good. This is about you having:

1. Better health now with security for yourself and your family later
2. Enjoyment, satisfaction, and fulfillment
3. More time to do what you want to do
4. Simpler choices
5. Comfort and vitality–now and through your retirement years
6. Looking and feeling great, reducing fat, and having tons of energy
7. Freedom from fear and worry–peace of mind

You see, I will show you how health really impacts every area of your life that is important to you. How your health is basically the same as your life. How, without health, none of the other areas matter. And how when your health is dealt with, many of the other areas of your life, many of the other things in your life, will just . . . fall into place.

It is like building a skyscraper. The first thing you have to do is get the idea, the spark that you want this building to exist. Then the location has to be found and cleared of any and all garbage. It must be cleared of anything that is going to get in the way of allowing the new building to be put up. When all the garbage, the old clutter, is cleared, now you can begin building, starting with the foundation, and working your way up.

This is what this book will do. This is what this book IS doing. It is empowering you to build your building of health, your body, mind and being of health, on a clear, solid foundation, so completely unshakable that it withstands the weathering storms and anything that comes its way. This will be your health, your wellness, unshakable, by the end of this book.

Your body and mind are not two different things. They are like two colors of a rainbow. Where does red stop and orange begin? In a rainbow, red doesn't stop, it merges into orange. There is no line. They are both frequencies within the same rainbow, just in a different place. The body and mind are the same way. There is no line. The body and mind are both frequencies of the same thing, a Human Being. We as humans made up the mythical line.

4

I point this out because it is impossible to separate the body from the mind. So there will be some things in this book that are borderline mind things. Enjoy them, realizing the body and mind are not two things; they are connected as one.

There are some major things that will be happening for you as I share with you what I have to share. And I want to share them with you, up front.

The first one is bringing you to a place where health is a natural expression for you. Where you do not have to "drag yourself out of bed" to be healthy, where you are not giving something up to be healthy, where you are doing what you want, and you still get to be healthy. Where health becomes a natural expression of who you are. Where health is effortless and easy.

I will leave you in a place where health is a natural expression for you.

I will help you get rid of the fear of ill health, eliminate the fear of sickness, and abolish the fear of death from disease. Knowledge is the key to eliminating fear. Part of what this book will do is to give you the knowledge to be able to completely eliminate fear. That is, to be at peace and harmony with your health, with your life. This will leave you in charge of your health, with you being the master of your destiny about health.

I will share with you how to actually be healthy, how to be well, and keep that health for the rest of your life. I will share with you what the keys are for doing this, which by the way, are easy simple, and usually free.

One of the other things I want to share with you up front is *desire*. You must create a desire that is so strong that you do not back down, so intense that it consumes you. I will help with this, and ultimately, it is your responsibility.

There is also some clarification that is needed about health, because there is so much information out there. Who is right? Who has the answers? What do you believe? If you believe everyone, you would not be able to do anything, eat anything, or say anything, because someone has made almost everything wrong or bad for you at some point or other. Or, if you believe everyone, you might end up doing anything, eating everything, and still expecting to be healthy.

Typical run of the mill knowledge is not going to cut it. There are so many books and so much information out there contradicting each other. Who do you believe, who do you trust? And most of that information is telling you what to do, or how to treat this, or how to treat that. This book will do none of that.

What do I have to share with you that is so different, that can make the changes that I am saying?

That is what you will find out by reading this book.

There are three sections to this book, and where you are at right now will determine where you will go first.

- If you want to be well, and you want to know whether what you are doing is healthy or not, then keep reading right through the book

- If you want to be well, be healthy, but have not seen the benefit, or been able to justify spending the time you "think" it takes to do so, keep reading, straight through the book

- If you don't see the benefit in being healthy, or even reading this book, go to Chapter 3, and then come back to here

- If you don't have the motivation to finish things and you know it is not likely you will follow through with everything in this book, go to http://www.bazuji.com and order my *Driving Forces and Values* CDs.

- If you are willing to do what it takes to be healthy, and just need some guidance on what to do, you can skip to Section 3 and then come back to here

- If you are in any other category I have not put here, just read straight through the book, twice.

I am STRONGLY recommending that you read this entire book, at some point, soon. The only difference is just where you should start and in what order you read it. Because health is more than just what you do, and that is what this entire book is about, how to have health and be well easily and effortlessly, for your entire life. No matter what.

If EVERY person in America read this book, 50% of our health care problems would be solved, 50% of the people would get healthier and better. Billions, if not *trillions* of dollars would be saved on health care costs alone.

If everyone in America actually DID what was in this book America's health care crisis would actually be solved. Ninety percent of all health problems would go away.

I cannot even imagine what would happen-wait, yes I can. People would be well, healthy. People would get along better, and understand each other better. People would be happier and more satisfied. People would feel better, and have more energy to do the things they wanted to do. People would think for themselves, instead of being controlled by fear, the media, and other people. It would be a society where everyone won. Imagine that.

The metaphors and repetition are not necessary for intellectual or conscious understanding. But if you read them, they will only go towards making what is in this book a natural expression of your life. You then don't even have to think about or even put much effort towards being well. So please, read it all. I promise by the end of the book you will naturally be living a life of health and well being and seeing the results manifesting in all areas of your life.

This book is not all perfectly grammatically correct, either. This will drive some people crazy. But this book is the way it is for one reason only: To produce the results I am promising. I use different nuances of the text (the stuff that some people see as wrong) to fully convey the message exactly as it would be conveyed if I were actually talking to you about this. Because, as we all know, text is very limited to how it can express something. It is easier to convey a message with the actual spoken word because you can say the same word so many different ways, often changing the entire meaning of a sentence. So for those of you who find all the little grammatical mistakes in everything you read, enjoy.

If you don't understand something, go back and re-read it. There are many ideas and ways of looking at things in here that you probably have never encountered before. It might take reading some of them twice before you understand them. Take the extra moment to go back and read again. It is your life we are talking about, and your life is worth it.

In Section 1, we will get really clear about what is real, what is so, as well as understanding what is made up, separating it from what is real. Now, that may sound simple, but you will see as we go through this, that there are many things people and the culture think are true that are not actually true.

In Section 2, we will show you how your thinking is the key to health, how your thinking is what will make the difference in your well being. Not what you do, or what you have, but how you think, who you are, in relation to your health and well being.

Section 3 is called "Who to be and what to do." I will show you how who you are will lead to what you are doing and, ultimately, to what you have: health and well being.

None of this is "the Truth." But it is the best thing that is available now. If you apply and do what is in this book, it will make a difference for you. So whether or not it is true, right, or wrong really isn't the question. It is a matter of will it make a difference for you? Will it help you more than anything else that is out there? And yes, I promise you, it will.

And I intend to make all of this fun for you. Fun for anyone who reads this book or to whom you give this book. To make it worth your while and time.

When children do something, they do it again and again; they keep doing it till they get it. They use the "mistakes" as a learning experience, as ways not to do it, until they find the way to do it. This is what we will do. Play at health, just like children. As humans, as adults, we tend to fall into the trap of "trying something once" and, if it doesn't work, then we give up. We need to get it "right" immediately, or we give up doing it, saying that we cannot do it, or we are no good at it or, even better yet, that we don't want to do it. From this point forward, I suggest you play at learning, like a child. Play at getting what you want, because when you play, you keep doing it, even if you don't do it the first time, or "fall off the wagon" or whatever. If you are being like a child, you just get back up and do it again, until you get it.

So without further ado . . .

SECTION ONE

Separating Reality from Myth

Chapter 2

The Four Biggest Myths

The Four Biggest Myths:
1. If you don't have symptoms, you are healthy
2. If you have symptoms, you are sick
3. If you want to be healthy, you have to do certain things (and you already "know" you cannot or don't want to do them)
4. When you get old, you become dependent on others and sick and diseased

These are all simply not true. They are not how it actually is; they are wrong.

First, what this chapter will do is dispelling the myths, and help you to understand the reality of it all. Because if you believe something is true that isn't, what you don't know CAN hurt you, and has been hurting you.

"If you don't have symptoms, you are healthy."
I will show you how this myth is not true first, because it is the easiest.

Look at the obituaries in any newspaper, and you will find at least one person who dropped dead of something—heart attack, stroke, etc.—and was reported to be in "perfect health." If they dropped dead, were they really in good health, even though they had no symptoms? Of course not; they were not healthy. And you will find people like this in almost every paper, almost every day.

Or how about when someone develops some serious symptoms within a couple of weeks, and they go to the doctor, and find out they have cancer? Before those couple of weeks when they got the symptoms, were they healthy? Obviously not. Just because you don't have symptoms doesn't mean you are healthy.

Now, because this might leave people a little fearful that they might die at any time, I need to address something here. It is all a matter of scale. Technically, you will not just suddenly die without any symptoms. You will have symptoms first; it is just that most people take so many symptoms as the status quo. They see so many symptoms as just part of life, part of getting old. But they are not.

For instance, low energy. Low energy levels are a symptom from your body, a symptom you are low on health. And many people just ignore it, because they write the symptom off as part of life, part of getting old, or whatever reason. When people are sad for no real reason, this is a symptom, and it does NOT have to be full blown depression, but just sadness. That is a symptom many people will also just write off. Headaches, back pain, neck pain, arm or leg pain, not being able to fall asleep within minutes, feeling cranky in the morning, bad eyesight, etc., etc. are more symptoms telling you that you are not healthy. The list of symptoms that we, as humans, generally write off as something else other than our body telling us we are not healthy, goes on and on.

Now, your body will always give you symptoms before you die. I promise. It is just that, as I talked about earlier, many of the symptoms you have, you don't even realize are symptoms. You just think that it is the way it has to be. Lack of energy, or not being fully awake and ready to go in the morning, or not being in a good mood most of the time, etc., are all symptoms that most of us ignore, because either we don't realize they are symptoms, or we think there is nothing the medical profession can do about them.

Not having symptoms does NOT mean you are healthy.

"If you have symptoms, you are sick."
Now I will show you how this big myth is NOT true either.

If you were choking on food, wouldn't you want to cough? It is a symptom that the body uses to get stuck food out of the airway or lungs. It is also a symptom that the body uses to get mucus and other garbage out of the lungs that it does not want - like during a cold.

If you get food poisoning and you throw up every half hour for hours or even days, do you want to stop throwing up? Yes, because it is no fun, but it is necessary for you to live. Does it seem unreasonable that even if you don't have food poisoning, throwing up might be a defense mechanism of the body?

By now, most people understand that a fever is a good thing, that the body creates the fever to help fight off sickness. Your body is creating the fever, voluntarily raising your body temperature. The fever is generally not a reaction to your environment, but the action the body takes to deal with the environment you have given it. Your body purposely gives you a fever for numerous reasons, some of which we probably don't know yet. Here, though are a couple:

With higher temperatures:
1. Many bacteria die; like a penguin in the desert, they cannot cope with the change in their environment
2. Chemical reactions happen quicker, and your body's response time is decreased. Remember in chemistry class, when you mixed stuff in the beakers, and when you increased the temperature, the reaction happened quicker?
3. P–54, interleukins, bradykinins, leukotrienes and other chemicals are released in the body. These chemicals are responsible for killing cancer cells in your body. I don't know about you, but I like that.

What about brain damage? I can almost hear you thinking that. Here is the scenario that almost ALWAYS happens when brain damage occurs from a fever:

The person, usually a child, gets a fever. The loving parents have been told this is bad and try to lower the fever with cold washcloths or aspirin. The fever goes down. On Day 2, since the body created the fever to help heal, it raises the body temp, but a little higher to make up for lost time. The parents then give the child Tylenol. The fever goes down. However, on Day 3 the fever goes up even higher because, again, the body is trying to heal with the fever. So, the parents give Extra Strength Tylenol. By this time the bacteria have done extensive damage and the body is getting "frustrated" trying to fend off the bacteria and having a hard time without the fever. So by Day 4, the fever goes way up, the parents get excited and bring the child to the ER. The doctors "know" that a fever is "bad" and give a prescription-strength fever suppressant. On Day 5, the body needs a fever, the bacteria are winning, and as a last-ditch effort the body is left with two choices… death or brain damage. So what do you think the body picks? The body raises the temperature to a level that causes brain damage, and the bacteria or whatever are finally under control.

It is not always this exact scenario. However, when brain damage is associated with fever, it is almost ALWAYS first suppressed chemically or with something cold. Fever is good. Fever is a symptom of your body healing, being healthy.

When you have diarrhea, a high number of cancerous cells can be found in your poop, sometimes a 50% increase in cancerous cells. So if your body is getting rid of extra cancer cells with diarrhea, maybe that is a good thing. I know it is not fun. But maybe your body is actually healing and cleaning house. Which is a good thing.

Bladder infections. Anyone who has had one, knows how much fun they are NOT. But maybe the symptoms of bladder infections are your body healing. First, there is having to go to the bathroom all the time. If there is no urine in the bladder, the bacteria will have no food. With no food, the bacteria die. Then there is the pain and discomfort. This just lets you know there is something wrong. It is a message from your body. Fever often goes with a bladder infection. And we already talked about all the benefits of fever, one of which is that some more bacteria just die. Then there is usually some blood in the urine. The body kills bacteria in the body in a couple ways. One of the ways is through direct contact with cells in the blood. White cells and other bacteria fighters float around in the blood, killing foreign things they bump into, including bacteria. But the problem is, you have no blood inside the bladder, no direct way for the body to kill the bacteria in the bladder. So your body opens up the walls between the cells, and lets some blood in, and in that blood are hordes of white blood cells that kill the bacteria. It is like the gates of a fort being opened. The army comes rushing through and all the little cells kill the bacteria in the bladder. Ingenious the body is.

Teething symptoms, symptoms of ear infections, and many more symptoms are often your body healing. Many symptoms, with a little knowledge of the body, can easily be explained as above as to how they are symptoms of the body healing.

So just because you have symptoms does NOT mean you are sick.

One of my most favorite stories is about trees.

Imagine, if you will, that it is fall, the leaves are starting to change colors, and some leaves are starting to fall from the trees. And out there in a group of trees, one of the trees, Ed the Tree, notices the other trees' leaves are turning colors. And Ed the Tree cringes and says to the other trees, "Eeewhh, get away from me, I don't want to catch what you have!" But no matter how hard Ed the Tree tries, he eventually "catches" what the other trees have, and even Ed's leaves begin to change colors. Then Ed the Tree notices that some of the other trees' leaves are falling off. And this time Ed will really try not to catch what the other trees have, because Ed does not want to lose his leaves. But, try as he might, Ed still "catches" what the other trees have, and Ed the Tree loses his leaves as well.

You are probably laughing to yourself, because of how silly Ed the Tree is. The leaves of all trees that live in climates with seasons change color and fall to the ground every autumn. Trees are part of nature. They do that.

Well, let me ask you a question. Are you part of nature? Are we as humans part of nature? Or are we separate from nature? Of course we are part of nature. We are mammals, just like all the other mammals on the planet. And just like everything else in nature, we as humans go through cycles with the seasons as well.

When the climate shifts from hot humid air to dry cold air, your lungs need a different lining to adapt to that new environment. You need different chemicals in your body to survive. You need to change, to adapt to the upcoming different environment. And when your body is not healthy enough, this change in your body gets expressed as a cold. You cough, and cough, and sneeze, and blow your nose, over and over again, to get rid of the old lining of your sinuses and lungs, which were designed for summer, in order to get the new lining ready to deal with the upcoming winter air. If your body is healthy enough, it can do this without your missing a beat. That is why some people never have the cold, and others, who have the cold, only have it mildly, and can go about their day-to-day activities with no problem.

Some people then say, "I always get my colds in the spring," or "I never get colds," as though trying to prove that colds are not a natural cycle of nature. Well, I ask you this, have you ever seen a tree in the winter with leaves? I have. Have you ever seen a tree lose its leaves in the spring? I have. Have you ever seen a tree that never loses its leaves? I have. We are part of nature. Your worrying about catching a cold or flu really is as silly as Ed the Tree's not wanting to catch the colors changing or his leaves falling off.

The trick is having enough health so that when it is time to change, you can do it with minimal discomfort and symptoms.

I love that little story.

So we know that not having symptoms does NOT mean you are healthy, and having symptoms does NOT mean you are sick.

This goes to show that the medical symptoms and disease care system is masquerading as health care. Eliminating symptoms and disease does not make you healthy. And since the medical symptoms and disease care system only *tries* to eliminate symptoms and disease, they are not actually health care. They are in fact medical symptoms and disease care. So if you don't have symptoms or disease, there is nothing they can do for you. They do nothing to increase your health.

Now I want to address the other two myths that are left: Getting old means you automatically lose your health and there are particular things you have to do to be healthy and well, and you already know you cannot or don't want to do those.

I don't blame you. If I had to do something I didn't want to do, or give up something that I really liked without anything else I really liked to replace it, I would probably not want to be healthy, either. I mean, for real, who would? I think this is one of the biggest reasons why so many people say they want to be healthy, but then do nothing about it. Because they think being healthy means some certain thing they do NOT want to do.

Here is one of the biggest secrets about being healthy and well:

EVERYONE is *different*! There is no one diet, there is no one exercise program or way of doing things that is right for everyone. You know, along with everyone else, that we are all different, yet almost NO ONE takes this into account when they dish out recommendations, or diets, or programs, or anything.

You are a special and unique individual, as is everyone.

I think that sums it up as well as anything.

We are all different, and yet the very fact we are all human gives us some similarities, and most people assume we are all the same, when it comes to recommendations and guidance. In fact, most people just recommend what worked for them, and the unique person that they are, assuming that what worked for them will work for everyone. Which we all know is not true. You have been there, done that, and some things you tried actually made you worse then before you did them.

You do NOT have to do certain specific things to be healthy and well. Some people will do great eating meat, and potatoes, and others will do well eating a vegetarian diet. It really depends on you, and I will get into that in more detail later. So relax, don't worry; I promised this would be fun and easy.

Growing old means you lose your health, and get decrepit and are dependent on other people.

This is also NOT true.

It is really simple to prove to you as well. The January 1973 issue of *National Geographic* featured an article entitled "Search for the Oldest People." In this article, they examined many different cultures, and hundreds of people who were well into their 100s, and almost all of them had the youth, freedom, clear mind, independence, and vitality of many people in their 50s here in the United States.

I am also going to share with you, in Chapter 16, how old age does not cause a lack of health and well being. But that is later.

To sum up the chapter:

Having symptoms does NOT mean you are sick.

Having no symptoms does not mean you are well.

Growing old and being old do not mean you are sick, diseased, and dependent on other people.

There is no one diet or one program for all people. Everyone is *different*.

Chapter 3

The Benefit and Hidden Cost of Health and Being Well

You probably are very familiar with the benefits you get from NOT being healthy. You get to eat food that tastes good, you get to be lazy and sit on the couch and veg out and watch TV. You get to not do all the hard work of exercise. There are many other benefits that people get from not being healthy, and many others that I probably did not list. I am not going to list them all, because you know most of them. I will list the benefits most people do not want to admit, often, even to themselves.

There are four main benefits that you probably get from not being healthy, that you don't want to admit:

1. Avoiding being responsible
2. Getting to be right and making others wrong
3. Dominating others and avoiding domination
4. Justifying yourself and invalidating others.

These things are the hidden benefits. I will talk about each of them in more detail, and explain what I mean. You have to dig down and be honest, though. These four things are usually true for everyone, and the point of my sharing them is to make you aware of them, and for you to be honest with yourself about them.

The medical symptoms and disease care system is responsible for your health. You don't have to do anything, and they will give you the magic pill to make you better. It is an illusion many of us want to believe. Because then we get to avoid being responsible for our own health. We get to do what we want, and then blame all of our symptoms on someone else.

You get to be right and do exactly what you want. You don't have to listen to all those doctors, all those people, especially that annoying "health freak" in your family. Every family usually has one. You get to be right about being able to do what you want. You get to make them wrong. And don't we all enjoy making someone we don't like so very wrong? Although it is not something most people want to admit, even to themselves.

You get to dominate others, and avoid others' dominating you. You do not have to do what they say. You can do what you want. You can probably even control people and make them angry by doing things your way, by doing what you want.

You get to justify yourself and invalidate others. You get proof for yourself that what you are doing is right. You get evidence that the way you are doing it is right. You get to make sure that other people's way of thinking is wrong, and make sure they know you know they are wrong.

These are the hidden benefits that many people get for not being healthy. Benefits that, if you are honest with yourself, you get as well.

What I am also going to point out is the not-so-obvious cost of not being healthy. There are benefits to being the way you are. But, as you know, nothing in life is free. If there is a benefit, there is a cost. What most people do not see is the cost, the price you have to pay for the benefits you are getting.

There are also tons and tons of hidden costs that most people never see. I will list some of the biggest ones. This is what it will cost you. This is what you will not have. You have to give up all of this to not be well. This is what it costs you to not be healthy:

1. Vitality
2. An abundance of energy to do everything you want to do
3. Happiness
4. Love and closeness with others
5. Satisfaction and fulfillment in life
6. Healing symptoms and disease
7. Symptoms and disease going away,
8. Relief from the suffering that goes with the symptoms and disease
9. Inner peace and harmony
10. Being symptom- and disease-free
11. Mental focus, memory, and clarity (no brain fog)
12. Being awake and fully alive every day (not just dragging through stuff and surviving)
13. Being present and having the ability to be with people
14. No worry or fear
15. Being confident in yourself
16. Being complete and happy
17. The ability to deal with issues that arise simply and with ease
18. Having better health now, with security for yourself and your family later
19. More time to do what you want to do
20. Simpler choices
21. Looking great, feeling good, reducing fat, and having tons of energy

The list goes on and on, but these are some of the big ones.

These are all things you do NOT get if you avoid being healthy. It is the price you have to pay to not be healthy.

If you are healthy, these are your rewards. These are the things you get when you are well. These things show up in your life as you are being healthy and well. So much so, that I want you to think of three other things vital to your happiness, freedom and life that you know you would get if you were well and healthy. Do it now.

In fact, put them on the next page, and move on when you think of three that apply to you, and/or your family.

1.
2.
3.

The list could really go on and on. So now, I will share with you what these costs really mean to you.

I will share a story with you about Bob. Bob wakes up in the morning fully rested and without an alarm clock. Bob gets up when his internal alarm clock naturally wakes him up, peacefully. Bob springs out of bed, excited and happy with what the day has to offer him. He is not grumpy, or in need of his coffee or other drugs to start the day. Bob feels great inside and is ready to go. Bob is not just a morning person either; his whole day goes like this.

Bob feels inner peace and is serene in all situations. Bob is able to deal calmly with all situations. He makes choices and does not look back or worry about them. Bob has time during the day to do everything he wants. He never says to himself "I don't have enough time." There is plenty of time, despite Bob's jam-packed full day.

Bob never gets even the slightest hint of headaches, back pain, neck pain, or any other kind of pain or allergies. Bob doesn't get slowed down by colds or flu. Bob is able to go as fast or as slow as he wants, because Bob doesn't experience symptoms.

Bob runs and plays for fun, like a kid. Because he can. Life is a game and a beautiful experience. Bob loves all people. No one crosses him or takes advantage of him. Bob demands respect and love from all people, and shows humility and respect for all people. Life flows gracefully for Bob.

Bob comes home at night with energy and zest for what the rest of the day has to hold, able to give everyone the love and attention they want. Bob goes to bed and falls asleep within minutes, sleeping soundly through the night until his internal alarm clock wakes him up.

This is what is possible. This is what it costs you to do things that don't add to your health. This is what you are giving up. Now, go back and look at the costs and benefits. Seeing for yourself, what would you rather have?

You have been choosing the benefits because the benefits are more immediate. The benefits are NOW! We live in a society of now people. We want everything now. Low monthly payments! No money down! Get it now! You deserve it! So we focus on what we get now, instead of what we will get now and in the future.

Of all the benefits of health and being well, here is my number one favorite…a great place to live. See, your body is where you really live. And if your body is not working, you will have no place to live. And I mean for real, not like being homeless on the street; without a healthy body, you will have no place to live.

When you are healthy and well, the place where you live is extremely comfortable. You don't have to worry about aches or pains. You don't have to feel weird, or out of sorts. When you are well, your home is a place to relax, and feel at ease. When you are well, your home can remain a beautiful home for your entire life.

Unlike the house you live in, your physical body is constantly repairing itself. Your body has a full-time handyman who knows how to do it all. All you have to do is not ruin your house faster than the handyman can fix it. That is really easy to do. The home of your body is designed to be able to keep you active, independent, and happy for at least 120 years, your entire life. There is not a preset time when your body will break down. It is not that the years of 65-75 will be bad, no matter what you do. You can be the same as when you were 30, if you want.

Health and well being are the number one priority for everyone. Including you. It might not seem like it, though. And I will show you what I mean.

Imagine you were diagnosed with this rare disease, and the only place there was a known cure was in Germany. Would you put your life on hold and go to Germany for the cure? Would you take time off from work, would you get the money, would you do what was necessary to go to Germany and get the treatment? Yes, of course; you would find the time and money. You would make everything work out.

Health is your number one priority. The circumstances just made you more aware of how health is the most important thing to you. When losing your health doesn't seem like an immediate threat, it is easy to put health and well being on the back burner. I wish doing things that added to your health always and every time had immediate gratification built in. I wish things that decreased your health had no benefits and your body immediately told you that what you just did was not good. Then it would be really easy to keep your health on the front burner.

Your health is the most important thing you have. We just kid ourselves that the things we do and don't do are not that big a deal, that they don't matter when, in fact, the choices you make every day are what determine how your life is going and where your life ends up.

If your health was forced in your face by some situation, you would be extremely determined to get better. Well, be that determined now. Be that committed now. What you will do by reading this book is bring yourself to a place where you want to do what it takes to be well now, where you are actually excited about being healthy.

The biggest obstacle that comes up for people being healthy is time. "I don't have enough time."

Let me show you how you don't NOT have enough time.

First, let's start off with the obvious. When you are sick and not feeling well, how productive are you? How much do you get done, compared to other days?

It takes time for you to be sick.

It wastes time when you are not as productive as you could be.

If you don't have any energy, do you think you will be productive, do you think you will get stuff done? Of course not. The energy you have is a product of how healthy you are.

Then there are days when you seem to get everything done. That has to do with your physical health, and how well your body operated.

These all add up to the reason why most people say they do not have enough time. They do not fully understand the full benefits of being healthy. Being healthy and well is more than just not having the cold or flu or how you feel. Being healthy and well is how everything in your body— and, as a result—everything in your life functions. If you get heartburn for two hours a day, that decreases your productivity. And heartburn is a

28

function of health. If you get headaches, or any kind of pain, that is a function of you not being healthy. If you get allergies or have vision problems, that is because you are not healthy.

Being healthy and well has so many more benefits than you probably realized. It is simply a matter of reminding yourself of all those additional benefits, and asking yourself if you are willing to give up these benefits for the immediate benefits you already know about? Are you willing to pay the cost?

Chapter 4

There is Not Just One Cause of Symptoms and Disease, and Treating Them Doesn't Work

This one is pretty straightforward, but it takes a bit to break up people's habitual ways of thinking.

First: There is no one cause of any symptom or disease.

For every symptom or disease, there are many different contributing factors. You have many different causes, or contributing factors, to any one problem. There is almost never just one cause.

Yet everyone is still looking for the one cause. What is the one cause? This is such an ingrained way of thinking that even natural health care providers fall prey to it. They look for the one cause of some symptom or disease. This way of thinking is accepted as the only way to do things. No one has ever really looked outside the box to consider that maybe there isn't one cause. Maybe what we need to do is look for all of the causes, all of the contributing factors, and deal with all of them.

We live in a society where cause and effect seem to be how the universe operates, as if there is some cause for every effect and there is only one cause for any one effect, when we all know there are many different contributing factors to any one effect. For instance, when it rains, how many different factors come into effect to determine whether it will rain or not? There are so many that weathermen still have a hard time predicting what the weather will do. There is not one cause of rain, or anything else in the universe for that matter.

An example of a symptom is dry mouth. How many different things can be contributing to having a dry mouth? Well, you could live in a dry climate like the desert. You could be dehydrated and not have enough water in your system. Your saliva glands might not be producing enough saliva.

For what possible reasons could your saliva glands not be producing enough saliva? Maybe the blood supply to the saliva glands is restricted. Maybe the ducts from the saliva gland are plugged, and it is not even a problem with the gland. Maybe the cell walls of the glands are not letting the saliva out. Maybe the nerves that control the glands are not working properly.

Well, why are the nerves not working properly? Why is the blood flow restricted? What could be causing the ducts to be blocked? How many things could cause the cell walls to malfunction?

Are you starting to see the complexity of something as simple as a dry mouth?

But people would not accept that complexity. They would do one thing to trying to "fix the problem" and, if it didn't work, they would quit doing it. For example, some people would try drinking water, or eat a low carb diet. And if that didn't work for them, they would quit doing it. They would quit because it "didn't work" and it obviously wasn't the one cause when, in reality, it was very likely a contributing factor to their problem.

Often, it is never just one thing that causes a problem. This is because the body has back-up system upon back-up system upon back-up system. If some part of the body has a job to do, there is almost always some back-up system to help make sure it is done correctly.

So even if there is a problem with one thing in the body, there is usually something else there to take its place, to do the job of that thing that is not working. So before you have a symptom or disease, there have to be multiple systems that are not working.

Often, it is a combination of many things that eventually leads to symptoms and disease. What the medical symptom and disease care system does is look for a single cause. What is the one cause of this problem?

As I said, this way of thinking, of looking for one cause, is so ingrained into our thinking that even natural health care providers usually do the same thing. Looking for the one cause is so accepted that it has never really been questioned until now, even by holistic and natural health care providers, and definitely not by the medical symptom and disease care system.

Some people, however, have been waking up to the myth of one cause. Some people have realized that something like a headache is just a label. That a headache in one person is probably caused by something different than a headache in another person. These people have put one foot over the boundary of the box and realized there is not the same cause in all people for the same symptom or disease.

If two people have the same symptom, a headache, they probably have different causes. Because they are different people, they probably have a different cause. But most practitioners are still looking for the one cause for every person.

Now we are taking it outside the box, beyond the boundaries, in that there is not one cause, even when talking about one individual. There are many different contributing factors to any symptom or disease.

Now, to be completely fair, what most have actually been looking for and not even known it is, What is the major contributing factor? What is the biggest factor that, if you "treat" it, will cause the symptom or disease to go away? Practitioners were unaware that what they were looking for was the major contributing factor.

One of the major problems with looking for one cause is, if something doesn't work, then it is usually written off as not the cause for this problem. But it might be, and probably is, a contributing factor. And if you get rid of enough contributing factors, the body will heal itself of the symptom or disease.

So when you shift your thinking to eliminating contributing factors, you can make progress in helping any person. And if you eliminate enough of the contributing factors, the body will then heal the symptoms and disease.

Let's take something a little more complicated. Headaches. What factors could be contributing to the symptom of headaches?

First, you could have restricted blood flow. And the restricted blood flow could be anywhere from the actual site of the pain to somewhere in the neck. You could have a problem with the nerves going into your head. You could have a problem with the fluid that flows around your brain bringing nutrients to the brain. What could be contributing to all of these things?

What could cause a restricted blood flow? It could be a result of bones and muscles not functioning properly, or plaquing of the blood vessels, or constriction of the blood vessels themselves. It could be due to chemicals that block the passage of blood out of the vessels, or weak muscles not being able to hold the blood vessels open. There may not ben enough ATP or energy for the valves to move the blood, or many, many other causes.

What could cause the nerves to be faulty? You could have a problem with the blood flow that supplies the nerves. You could be missing chemicals that are needed for the nerve transmission to go through the nerve. You could have too much of these chemicals. The nerve could be dehydrated and not have the proper water/chemical balance for the nerve impulse. The nerve could be damaged from not being able to repair itself. There are, again, tons and tons of things that could cause a nerve to not function properly.

What could cause the fluid around the brain to be interfered with? As this is the fluid that brings energy to the brain, and gets rid of the waste products, you could have bones in your head that are stuck. You could have restricted breathing. You could just not be breathing deeply. There could be not enough water for the fluid, and it is thick and sludgy and doesn't move properly. There could be a blockage in the passage ways where this fluid moves. And many more.

And we can take every thing in the above three paragraphs as possible contributing factors to headaches, and produce another paragraph of all the possible causes of each of them. And we could find even more causes for each of these new causes. It literally could go on for a long time.

There is no one cause. There is always a combination of many of these things that leads to headaches in someone. And if you address enough of these contributing factors, the body will heal, and the headaches will go away.

This scenario is exactly the same with all symptoms and disease. There is no one cause of any symptom or disease. There are many contributing factors. Some are bigger factors than others. And there is definitely no one same cause of any symptom or disease in different people. We are all unique individuals, and have our own set of life circumstances and body/mind/spirit functions that create any one symptom or disease. There is no same one cause for different people.

That is why the medical symptom and disease care system has yet to really find a cure for almost anything. One hundred years of glorious medical symptom and disease care, and almost no cure for anything. And when I say "cure," I do not mean taking some medication repeatedly for the rest of your life. That is managing symptoms and disease, not curing it.

The top 13 leading causes of death in America that are symptom and disease related prove this. If medical practitioners had a cure for something, it would not kill people who could get the cure. Yet almost 1.5 million people die every year from the top 13 causes of death alone. And there are thousands and thousands of known symptoms and diseases that can and do kill people.

Could this possibly be because the medical symptom and disease care system is still looking for the one cause, the one cause for each labeled symptom and disease for all people and the one cause, not all the contributing factors? Maybe if the medical symptom and disease care system began to accept what almost everyone else knows, they might make a positive difference. But you do not have to wait for them to finally catch on.

You can begin eliminating known possible contributing factors now. You can realize that you are not looking for one cause, but are looking for contributing factors. You can keep in mind that a label, symptom, or disease does not tell you anything about your special set of contributing factors. You are different, and your label will usually not provide any insight into what your contributing factors are. I want to make it clear that I am not saying it won't, I am saying it probably won't.

I also want to make the distinction here between symptoms and disease.

Symptoms will often give you great feedback. As I will talk about in Chapter 7, symptoms can be helpful. Diagnosis of a disease almost never is helpful.

What is a disease? What is a diagnosis? It is someone having certain symptoms. They then get a certain diagnosis or disease label to go with those symptoms. One example, fibromyalgia, is a really easy way to explain exactly what I mean.

Most people have heard of fibromyalgia. To get a diagnosis of the disease labeled "fibromyalgia," you have to have widespread pain in most of your body, and 11 tender points coinciding with the 18 points on a chart. Then medical practitioners will label you with fibromyalgia.

I have a question. What are the contributing factors to widespread pain? How many different things do you think can cause widespread pain? Many. And how many different things can cause tender points in your muscles? Again, many. So even though there are probably at least thousands of things that can lead to the symptoms that indicate fibromyalgia, the medical profession still groups all people with these symptoms into the same category, with the diagnosis of fibromyalgia, and then proceeds to look for the one cause of fibromyalgia and, therefore, the one cure.

This is what they do for almost every diagnosis.

Diabetes is uncontrolled blood sugar levels higher than average. (I will talk about average and normal in Chapter 7 as well.) So what can cause blood sugar levels to be higher than average? Well, for starters, your body makes and releases chemicals that actually raise blood sugar levels. I bet you that if people actually bothered to check, many people with the diagnosis of diabetes actually produce too much of these other chemicals, and has nothing to do with a lack of insulin.

The liver's job is to monitor the level of blood sugar, or glucose in the blood. So if the monitoring device is off, how well can the actual level be maintained? Not very well. The liver is kind of like the gas gauge of your car. The gauge doesn't cause low or lots of fuel. It just gives you feedback, so you can keep appropriate levels of fuel in your car. If the gas gauge is broken, it makes it tougher to know how much fuel is in the car.

Blood glucose levels must be maintained in a much narrower range than the gas in your car. So imagine trying to always have between 6.5 and 7 gallons of gas in your car at all times, with a broken gas gauge! It would be hard enough with a working gauge. Well, if the liver is not monitoring the blood glucose properly, of course there will be problems.

And these are only a couple of possible other contributing factors. There are many. Yet the medical symptoms and disease care system is still looking for the one cure for the one cause. This will never work.

Every disease has many, many different contributing factors to the symptoms that led to the diagnosis. And each person has different contributing factors in different amounts that led to their symptoms and ultimate diagnosis.

What you can do is look for contributing factors, and begin eliminating them, knowing that there are multiple contributing factors that are usually unique to you.

Now, do not be overwhelmed with thinking about "how am I supposed to find all these contributing factors, when they are always different in different amounts?"

If you wanted to treat symptoms and disease, you would have to get good at this game of contributing factors. I am pointing this out because I do not see a way to make the medical symptom and disease care system quit treating symptoms. I see shifting the focus to contributing factors as a step that they can actually do. And maybe they actually might.

In the later chapters, I will give you really simple, in fact ridiculously simple, ways to help you be healthy and well, so that your body can heal itself of the symptoms or disease you have without your having to know anything about diagnosis, symptoms, or the millions of different ways to treat things.

I will give you a way you can personally ensure your continued health and well being, a way you can ensure that your later years are as good as the early years. And it is simple. Really simple.

Now, the second thing. Treating symptoms, and why not to treat symptoms. The most common and obvious reason is that the symptom is not the problem. The symptom is the warning signal that something is wrong, that you need to do something. If all you do is treat the symptom and try to get rid of the symptom, you almost never do anything about the actual problems going on in the body. If you have a backache and take aspirin hoping the pain will go away, this is treating the symptom, and not doing anything about the problems that are contributing to the pain.

If you take insulin for diabetes, that is treating the symptom, the symptom of your blood sugar being too high, but it is doing nothing to deal with the contributing factors that are causing the blood sugar levels to be too high.

If you take antibiotics for an infection, it is doing nothing about the contributing factors to why the infection is there in the first place.

Now, I want to be very clear about this. I am NOT saying don't take aspirin, or don't take insulin, or don't take antibiotics. They are great tools to TEMPORARILY help out a situation until the contributing factors can be dealt with. They are not long-term solutions to anything.

I will go into this in more detail in later chapters, but it needs to be brought up here as well. I am not saying don't treat symptoms. Caring for people and using their symptoms to help you figure out what the contributing factors are can be useful.

Health is more than the absence of symptoms and disease. Even if you are able to treat all the symptoms and make the disease go away, it still does not mean the person is healthy. It only means they don't have the symptom or disease at that time.

Where I am coming from is eliminating the need for all of that, because my goal is that no one will have symptoms or disease to be treated, as in the disclaimer in the front of my book. And, yes, it is totally possible to be completely symptom- and disease-free. I am even talking about those nuisance symptoms that many people just put up with, like low energy, or bad moods, or lousy relationships, or mediocre sex, or aches and pains. All of these are symptoms, and none of them have to ever be experienced.

Be cautious when treating symptoms and disease. Treating them is usually doing nothing about the contributing factors and what is behind the expression of the symptoms and disease.

Realize that there is no one cause for any one problem, and that the contributing factors for even the same symptoms or disease in different people is always different. There may be some that are the same, and the contributing factors and combinations of them are different for different people.

Chapter 5

Viruses, Bacteria, and Parasites Do Not Make You Sick

Many people fear symptoms and disease because they think that the outside world makes you sick, that you catch things from viruses, and that bacteria make you sick. This is simply not true. It is just a big myth that viruses cause colds, flu and disease. Bacteria cause infections, strep, and sore throats. Parasites cause malnutrition, etc. All of these are myths. Not true.

I know this flies in the face of common belief about viruses and bacteria. A little history is in order here.

Louis Pasteur came up with the germ theory in the early 1800s. He said that he believed germs cause disease. Near the end of his life, it is said that Pasteur proclaimed: "the terrain is everything." Simply put, this was an admission that the true cause of disease is the internal environment of you, not the bugs, viruses and bacteria inside you. It is the state of your internal health, the terrain, which either allows for germs to invade and injure the organism or fends them off. In other words, viruses do not make you sick. You have to have a weak body before you will get sick.

Most of the evidence that is used to support this theory that even the father of this theory said wasn't true, is that the virus is found wherever the sickness is. When someone has pneumonia, the pneumonia virus is present. When someone has the flu, the flu virus is present, and so on. Since the virus is present every time the sickness is, that is the "proof" that the virus causes the disease or that the bacteria cause the illness.

Most people fear, worry, or are concerned to some degree (all similar things, different shades), about catching something—some virus, bacteria, parasite, or something—because they have been led to believe that these microbes, viruses, bacteria and parasites, cause sickness.

Let me tell you why microbes do not cause sickness. First, let's go back to what I pointed out in an earlier chapter, i.e. that there is not one cause for anything. The bootstrap theory of quantum physics shows us that everything is interconnected and interdependent, and that there is not one cause, but infinite causes, with some being major contributing factors, and other minor contributing factors. So at best viruses, parasites, and bacteria are major contributing factors to sickness. But they are not even this. They are barely contributing factors to sickness.

Let me ask you a question. If the viruses caused, or were even major contributing factors to disease, and if you had a virus inside you, you should have some sickness or disease that the virus "causes," right? You might be surprised to know that you have all different types of viruses and bacteria inside you right now. You probably have a couple of cold viruses, a couple of flu viruses, and probably a couple of strep viruses in you also. And yet, you are not expressing any sickness or disease "caused" by those viruses.

It stands to reason that if you have a virus inside of you, and yet you do not have the "sickness it causes," then obviously viruses alone do not cause the sickness.

Consider something a little closer to home that you can directly relate to. Take a family that has three kids. Each time someone gets sick, only one or two end up getting sick. If the virus is really spread and caught, wouldn't all members of the family get the cold or flu, or whatever virus is going around? They are in close intimate contact. Even better, take a couple—one gets sick, and the other doesn't, even though they were touching, kissing, and only God knows what else.

I have another little story.

If you were to take a trip to all the garbage dumps around the world, at every single dump you would find the same thing. At every garbage dump in the world you will find rats. Every single one. So if you follow the traditional thinking, then, since everywhere there is a garbage dump you find rats, then rats must cause the garbage dump, right? Rats are what "cause" the garbage dump to be there.

It is obvious the rats do not cause the garbage dump.

Yet, because viruses are attracted to the dump in the human body, common thought seems to think the virus caused the sickness or the disease.

Some then say, yeah, why do different diseases and different sicknesses have different viruses associated with them? It is simple.

Ants flock to sugar, rats to garbage, flies to poop, and bees to nectar. Just as in nature, different viruses are attracted to different dumps in the body. We all have different genetic strengths and weaknesses. When one part of our body gets weak, the viruses that are attracted to that weakness grow and spread, just like ants to sugar, rats to garbage, dogs to meat, etc.

There is a principle in quantum physics called the holographic universe. What this means in plain English terms is that there is a reflection of the whole in each part. The larger parts are like the smaller parts. And this can be found on many levels. Just as in looking at the larger picture of how the universe works, so it is within our body. As you know, we humans are also part of nature. So, as in nature, different critters are attracted to different things, different viruses are attracted to different weaknesses in our body.

Most people have heard that there are good bacteria in the body. Many bacteria in your intestines are not only good, but needed for your survival.

There are more bacteria on one square inch of your skin than there are people on the planet. There are more different types of bacteria in your body than there are people on the planet. Bacteria make up 10% of the dry weight of your body. If you didn't have bacteria on your skin, your skin would have fungus growing everywhere, and you would probably be dead.

Not only do bacteria not cause sickness, but they are needed for your health and survival. Twenty years ago, no one really knew there were good bacteria. Twenty years ago, people believed that all bacteria were bad. How much longer before we find out viruses and parasites are also beneficial and needed for our survival? I promise you, just as bacteria were once all thought to be bad, it is only a matter of time before we find out that there are also good viruses and parasites. It is only a matter of time.

Viruses, bacteria, and parasites do not cause sickness and disease. They are only small contributing factors. Our bodies have to be in a weakened state first. Our health has to be at a low level, and then the viruses take advantage of the opportunity and we get sick. To repeat, they are like ants at a picnic. The ants would not be there if there were no sugar. The rats would not be at the dump if there were no garbage. The flies would not be around poop if there were no poop. The viruses, bacteria, and parasites would not be making you sick, if there were no sick body. You already have to be sick before the viruses, bacteria, and parasites can do anything.

Chapter 6

Your Genes Do Not Dictate Your Health

Contrary to popular opinion, your genes do not control your body. They do not dictate your health and well being, your personality, or anything. They are a contributing factor to your health and well being. They are a contributing factor to your personality and your life.

It goes back to the age old psychological question. Is it our nature that dictates who we are or is it how we are nurtured? Said another way, is it our genes, or how we are raised that dictates who we are? Well, I say it is both. They both are factors in determining what happens. Not only with how one behaves, but with how our body responds to the environment. How healthy we are. How we think and how smart we are.

The good news with this is nothing is set in stone. Your genes are not something that cannot be changed. Your genes are not the way it is, and there is nothing you can do about it. Your genes can be shaped and molded. In fact, your genes are shaped and molded throughout your life time. In fact, on a daily basis. Your genes are constantly changing on a daily basis.

The best place I have seen this put together in one place is by a cellular biologist named Bruce H. Lipton, Ph.D. www.brucelipton.com. Most of the facts and some of the ideas I have in the rest of this chapter are based on Bruce Lipton and the sources he sites.

In order for you to understand that your DNA is not the major contributing factor in determining anything in your life, I am going to explain a little about your cells and how they work. To understand how your body and cells actually work is really quite simple. Especially if you know computers.

First, proteins are what make you and me able to walk, talk, think, and do everything we do. These are not to be confused with protein in regards to diets and fats and things like that. They are much smaller, select chains of amino acids. The protein that most people talk about with diets is actually made up of the smaller proteins I am talking about here. These small proteins are what make animal behavior and physical expression possible.

The cells in your body contain the exact same systems as your entire body. Each cell in your body has a respiratory system, digestive system, skin system, nervous system, muscle and bone system, immune system. They are different in the parts that make them up, but they do the same thing. And the proteins are what allow these systems to work at the cellular level.

Scientists have known about this for a while. Since they know the brain and nervous system are what controls your body, they began looking for the brain of the cell. What controls the production and governs these proteins. What is the brain of the cell?

In 1956 the structure of DNA was discovered and found to be the blueprint for making these proteins. That all the proteins in the body where made from the DNA of the cells in the body. So it was then automatically assumed, without any studies or anything, that the DNA is then the brain of the cell. And for almost 50 years, has been assumed to be true. Nothing proving this or backing it up other than the DNA is where the proteins for life get made. So it must be the brain and controlling center of the cell.

Ok, they actually had Darwin's theory that had been in acceptance for almost 100 years to back up this train of thought. You know, survival of the fittest. The cells have random genetic mutations, and the mutations and traits that are better for survival, pass this trait along. And the fittest survive. But there still where no studies to try and prove this theory. It was just accepted. And has been generally accepted as true by most people up until this point.

Then in the 90's when they actually started doing studies, everything seemed to point to the DNA not being the brain of the cell.

The first was when some guy said, well, if the DNA is the brain of the cell, then if we take out the brain, the cell should die shortly thereafter. And when they removed the DNA from the cells, the cells lived. They did not die. In fact they went on living a normal life, doing everything they did up until the point the cell would have normally died. Then the cell died. So it was shown, over and over again, if the DNA is removed, the cell continues to function. This means the DNA is not the brain of the cell.

So what is? This is the question that people began to ask. And what they found is the cell wall and the receptor/effector sites in the cell wall were actually the brains of the cell. The cell wall is what keeps the stuff on the outside of the cell out, and what keeps the stuff on the inside of the cell in. Unless the cell wants to move something across that membrane.

The receptor/effector sites are actually how the cell communicates with the environment. The receptor/effector sites are how the cell is able to respond and take appropriate action based on the environment. The receptor/effector sites are how the cell grows and does all the processes necessary for life. And most importantly, the receptor/effector sites are how the cell actually activates and turns on the DNA to duplicate and do its job.

That last line is very important. The cell wall receptor and effectors actually are what turn on the DNA. So the fact that there is something that controls the DNA is actually then what controls the cell. The perceived environmental signals through the cell receptor/effector sites are actually what determine what the cell is going to do and not do. What controls and regulates the cells. The receptor/effector sites of the cell wall are actually the brains of the cell.

So again, if you take away the brains of the cell, the cell should stop functioning. People took away the cell receptor/effector sites, and that is exactly what happened. The cell died shortly thereafter.

And the interesting part about all of this is the environment is the main thing which actually stimulates the receptor/effector sites. The *perception* the cell has of the environment determines how the cell behaves. The key word in that sentence is perception. It is the perception of the environment the cell has, not how the actual environment is. The perception and actuality of the environment can be the same, but are not automatically the same.

A biochemical definition of the cell membrane reads as follows: the membrane is a liquid crystal, semiconductor with gates and channels. This definition is exactly the same as that used to define a computer chip. Recent studies have verified that the cell membrane is in fact an organic homologue of a silicon chip. There are analogies and homologues. Analogy is a similar comparison. Like comparing rats at the dump to viruses and your health. They are similar. A homologue is the same thing. Not similar, but the same. And the cell membrane is the same as a computer chip.

This is where knowing computers make it a little easier than it already is to understand how the cells and your body actually work.

The cell walls are the brains or the processor of the computer. The DNA is like the hard drive. The DNA stores all the programs and information about how to make you and your life. Your hard drive does not control the computer, but is the storage of information about everything your computer does. The same is true of the DNA of the cell.

Your keyboard and mouse are the inputs that actually make your computer do something. The keyboard and mouse access stored information on the hard drive, and that determines what the computer actually does. The receptor and effector sites in the cell wall are like the keyboard and mouse. The receptor and effector sites actually get input and stimuli from the environment. This input determines what the cell does.

The hard drive of your computer has different parts. One part of the hard drive is the information you do not want to change. This is the operating system, like windows and other programs you use. If you change this part, the whole computer gets messed up. There is another part of the hard drive that stores the information, or programs, on how to repair the hard drive if something happens to it. Then there is a part of the hard drive that stores information temporarily and is what the computer uses to do things short term. And the last part of the hard drive has information or programs that can actually change and install new programs.

Now, the DNA of your body is exactly the same. You have 4 parts to your DNA. (That we know of so far).

1. The main part of your DNA has all the history of you and the evolution that led up to you. Everything that is needed to make an entire you is encoded onto the DNA of every single cell. Every cell has the complete DNA to make every other type of cell that makes up you. That is why they can clone animals from one cell. This DNA includes all the changes that have gone on to your DNA since you were conceived as well.

2. Another part of your DNA is the proofreader. It makes sure that the DNA is correct, copied correctly, and everything is functioning fine.

3. You also have a part of your DNA that is like a temporary store house of changed DNA and information. This part is what the cell uses to determine right now, what other parts of your DNA are going to be copied and replicated.

4. And the last part is the most interesting part. It is the part of your DNA that actively and purposely alters your DNA to deal with the perceived environmental circumstances. You actually have DNA to creatively and constructively create new, never been around before, DNA. This DNA is the cell adapting and changing with purpose and intent to better deal with the environment.

This was shown by a study where bacteria, which have a very similar cell structure to humans, actually specifically mutated with intent. Under conditions where random mutations could not have happened. The bacteria changed their DNA with purpose and intent, to help them better adapt to the new environment they were in. This means two HUGE things.

Even though you were born with a certain DNA, you can change it. In response to your perception of a different environment, you can change your DNA. Your body can with purpose and intent change your DNA to make you better able to adapt to the environment. That means your genes do not control your health. Your perception of the environment has a bigger impact on your genes and health than does your DNA

Two, that the Darwinian Theory is wrong. The universe did not come about by spontaneous random mutations and the fittest survived. But that there is some intelligent force behind the specific evolution with intent and purpose. That evolution has been happening consciously.

I want to go back to the perception part for a bit. Because this is huge when it comes to your life, as well as your health and well being.

What the cell perceives from the environment is what it responds to. This may or may not be the same as the actual thing in the environment. Let me explain.

Most of your cells have an environment of you. Their outside environment is only more of you. Meaning, most of your cells only respond to signals from your brain or endocrine system. And the endocrine system is also controlled by your brain. So directly or indirectly, all the cells on the inside of your body, which are most of the cells in your body, respond to signals from your brain.

And your thoughts and belief systems alter and change the signals your brain sends to your body. Let me give you an example. You are walking down the street, and you see a snake. What do you do? Your brain gives all sorts of feedback to your body on how to prepare for what you are about to do. Then, right before you do whatever it is you were going to do, you realize the snake is really only a piece of rope. Then what do you do? Your brain prepares and sends all new information to your cells about what they should now do.

When you thought the rope was a snake, your cells were responding to a false perception. They were acting according to the perception that happened, and not the actual event that happened in reality, a rope. Your physical misperception affected how you, your cells, and your being responded.

Here is the interesting part. Your belief systems about snakes, which you never consciously thought of, are what determined that action you were about to do. Most little boys and the crocodile hunter would have run up to check out the snake. Many adults would just be careful, a little on the defensive and cautious side, and walk around the snake. And many other people would scream and run in panic. Your underlying belief of what snakes are, determines your action with out you even thinking about your beliefs. If snakes are cool and interesting you automatically go and check the snake out. If snakes are bad and dangerous, you use caution. If snakes are deadly poisonous creatures out to get you, you scream and run in the other direction. Your beliefs determine the response your cells have.

You have a belief, snakes are whatever. Then when you saw a snake, your brain automatically accessed that belief system, and sent the not so appropriate information to the cells in your body to respond a certain way.

Let's say you believe viruses make you sick. Then when someone sneezes on you your brain accesses that belief system, without you even knowing about it. Then sends the inappropriate response to your cells about what to do, based on your belief system. If you believe that viruses make you sick, then when someone sneezes on you who is sick, you are much more likely to become sick.

If you believe the cancer is really hard to get rid of. Then if you ever are told you have cancer your brain will access that belief system, without you even being aware of it, and your cells will respond to the inappropriate message. You will have a hard time healing the cancer, because of your belief systems.

This really applies to everything in your life. If you believe life is hard, it will be. Because life happens, your brain will access that belief system, and will send the inappropriate signals to the body, making life hard.

Women are too emotional, men are jerks, can cause the same thing. You will end up proving to yourself, that any belief system you have is true. Because the cells will respond to the signals from the brain, which are altered by the belief systems you have.

I am going to be going into this more in my next book, *The Creators Manual for Your Mind*, but I think you are beginning to see the far reaching affects of this.

This is why so much of this book is dealing with your faulty belief systems. Even if my logic is flawed, even if my reasoning does not stand the test of time, having belief systems that empower you and make it easier to be healthy, help. That is why I said in the beginning, it is not a matter of right or wrong, true or false, but what works. And this stuff works.

There is actually a physical measurement for how your belief systems change your cellular response in the body. Your cells will actually change and adapt to the perceived conditions. You will get more receptor/effector sites the more you use them. Just like your muscles. The more you work out and use your muscles, the more muscle you will get. The more you use specific receptor/effector sites, the more of them you will get. And the more of them you get, the easier it is to set them off.

Said another way. You can build up lots of "the environment is hostile" receptor/effector sites. So much, that any little thing will set them off. And it becomes easier and easier to find the hostile environment. If you believe the environment is hostile, you will eventually end up proving it to yourself. Your misperceptions and experience will be the environment is hostile. Because you will have more of those type of receptor/effector sites.

The opposite is also true. You can build up, the world is great and everyone is wonderful receptor/effector sites. And it becomes easier and easier to see the good in the world. To see the good in people. Either way, there actually is a measurable difference in the number of receptor/effector sites the more they are used.

Something even more interesting is that a cell is binary, like the computer. Either off or on. But in the case of the cell, the cell is either growing or protecting. The cell cannot do both. If the environment is perceived as hostile, the cell goes into defensive mode and is not growing or healing. If the environment is perceived as friendly, the cell is stimulated into the growth and healing cycle. It is either one or the other.

What this means is if you are in constant fear, stress and worry, your cells can do nothing but stay in protection mode. Now every cell is designed to cope and deal with being in the protection mode. But when the cells of your body are mostly in the protection mode, they cannot heal, they cannot grow, and they cannot repair themselves from damage. Said another way, if you are fearful, perceiving a hostile or threatening environment, you cannot heal or grow.

If you are fearful of someone attacking you, taking your kids, terrorists attacking, losing your job, not paying the bills, or anything, you are not healing and growing. If you are worried about the company you work for, or your family, or your children, or what you should do with the relationship you are in, you are not growing. You are in the protection mode. When you experience jealousy, hate, or anger, you are in the protection mode. You are not healing or growing. If you fear death, you are ironically bringing yourself closer to death.

Your perception and beliefs play a huge role in your health and well being. Your DNA does not control your health or life. You do. Your DNA does not dictate who you are, the emotions you experience, or the world around you. You do. Your mind does. Your perception does. Your beliefs do. And this means, change your mind, and change your world. This book is shifting how you view the world of health. How you see things. And thereby shifting your actual health.

That is partly what I mean by having health be a natural expression with very minimal extra effort. You change your belief systems, and it will automatically change your response. Beautiful.

Chapter 7

What Symptoms and Disease Really Mean

First, I need to tell you about the difference between "average" and "normal."

Average is a mathematical statistic. Don't let that big M word scare you. All average means is that you add up all the totals you have and divide by the number of totals you added. This gives you an average of the group of numbers.

Normal is what is right for an individual, or what is common or appropriate for a particular person.

What the medical profession does is make the average normal. They measure a bunch of people's blood pressure, divide the added totals by the number of people they measured, and come up with an average blood pressure. And then they say this is the normal blood pressure for everyone.

I will let you in on a little secret. If you had the blood pressure I have at this exact moment, you would probably pass out. If you had the same blood pressure standing as you did sitting, you would probably pass out. Your blood pressure changes all the time, all day long. Your normal blood pressure needs to be different than everyone else's. You need the right blood pressure for you at the right time. If you had the average blood pressure all the time, you probably would be dead by now.

Just because some numbers are the average does not mean they are normal. Everyone is different. Everyone knows this, it seems, except the medical symptom and disease care system. They seem to think we should all have the same numbers; otherwise there is something wrong with us.

And on top of that, the medical symptom and disease care system even changes what is supposedly normal with time. "Normal" depends on what year it is. Maybe this is because there is no normal for everyone. There is only a normal for you. What the medical profession says is normal is actually the average.

And you know, when dealing with averages, that not everyone is the average number. Just as in school, with the bell curve, the average might be a "C," but there are people who got "As" and those who got "Fs." Does that mean that just because the people who got "As" are not in the average, there is a problem with them, something is wrong? Of course not. And contrary to what many people will immediately think, someone who got an "F" does not automatically have a problem, either. Maybe they were absent, and that is their current grade. Maybe the grade is in gym, and they will be the next Bill Gates, so physical conditioning is not important to them. Maybe they forgot about the test and didn't study. The "F" might be a signal of something potentially wrong. It does not automatically signal a problem.

This is the same with the averages and normals the medical profession uses. The averages can serve as guideposts to maybe show a sign of some potential problem. The problem is that the medical symptom and disease care system uses the averages *as* normal, and if you are not normal, it *is* a problem, as they see it. They forget that the numbers are only averages, that everyone is different, and that your normal might be completely different than the average. For you, that normal is perfectly healthy, even though it is not average.

So what do you do with this? Take all the numbers the doctors give you with a grain of salt. Just because their charts show you "should be" in this range does not mean you actually should. You are different than everyone else. Your normal might be outside of the range of average they go by and still be perfectly healthy for you.

This brings up a show on the Discovery Channel about a culture and group of people in Italy. They had an average cholesterol level of well over 300. Yet, almost none of them had any heart problems or plaquing what-so-ever. The whole show was about trying to figure out why. Well, at the end of the show, they had no real answer. Only theories. Well, how about this one? How about their normal was perfectly healthy for them? That the average is just that, an average that not everyone will fit into.

Good. Now on to what else symptoms mean. There are three different types of symptoms: symptoms of the body healing, symptoms of the body reacting to the environment, and symptoms of the body's innate wisdom communicating with us directly. The first two types of symptoms have two roles, as they are also messages about what is happening. So how do you know which symptoms are what?

It doesn't matter. Because all symptoms are messages from your inner wisdom, and that is all that matters. When you get the message, when you listen to what your inner wisdom is telling you and act, the symptoms will often go away.

Symptoms are your body yelling at you. Your body is a beautiful thing. It is like a little kid. A little kid will say something to you, and if they don't get your attention, they will get louder and louder until you pay attention. Your inner wisdom communicates to you through your inner knowing all the time. And when you don't listen to the messages from your inner knowing, your body speaks louder.

First your inner wisdom will communicate with you directly. It will tell you to exercise, but you might say you are too tired. Your inner wisdom might tell you to go to bed, but you really want to watch the last part of a TV show. It might tell you to quit eating because you are full, but you really like the food and were taught to clean your plate, so you keep eating. It goes on and on. Your inner wisdom tells you what to do, and often you don't listen.

Then you get little symptoms, symptoms that many people just deal with, like low energy and fatigue, being grumpy or worrying, and many other little things that are so common, people think they are normal. These are early warning signs, signals from your body that are a little louder, because you were not listening. And when you ignore these, they get even louder. You get symptoms like aches and pains, headaches, high blood pressure, high cholesterol, and allergies, plus many other symptoms. These are symptoms that some people still ignore. Many just don't know these symptoms are their inner wisdom telling them something, telling them what they are doing is destroying the health of their body.

Then, if you don't listen, or don't know to listen to these messages, they get even louder. You get some label, a diagnosable disease-arthritis, Alzheimer's, a heart attack, stroke, cancer or something of the sort. This is your body yelling, screaming at you, trying to tell you what it has been saying all along: "What you are doing to me is killing me. Quit it!"

Now, just because you are expressing symptoms doesn't mean you are sick.

The three types of symptoms again: symptoms of your body actually healing. Some symptoms are reactions to the environment and what is happening. Some symptoms are nothing more than a direct communication, created by your innate wisdom and body, to get what it wants. All of these symptoms are still giving you feedback about what the environment and your belief systems about the environment are doing to you. More specifically, what your inner wisdom wants you to do about it.

In fact, all symptoms are your body and inner wisdom communicating with you, no matter which group they belong to. They are "messages" if you will, that something is wrong, that something needs to be done differently, or stopped altogether.

And it doesn't matter which group the symptoms fit into, because all symptoms are just feedback, feedback our body is giving us about what is happening. You don't have to know which type of symptom it is, you just have to be aware of the feedback. And the feedback is obvious.

For instance, if you eat spicy food and you get heartburn, don't eat spicy food. It is that easy. But no, we as humans know better, so we take antacids and, even better, we take medications ahead of time when we eat foods we know are not going to sit right with our bodies.

It is as if you hit yourself on the head with a hammer, and it HURTS. So you take some aspirin. Then you hit yourself on the head with a hammer again, and it hurts, so you take some more aspirin. The next time you get smart. Before you hit yourself on the head with a hammer, you take some aspirin, so it won't hurt as much when you actually hit yourself on the head with a hammer. How about you just quit hitting yourself on the head with a hammer?

The only difference between this and many other symptoms, is that you get some benefit, some pleasure out of doing what causes the symptom. And it is what you are doing that eventually leads to the symptom. Many people just want the pain or whatever the symptom is to go away so they can keep the pleasure, so they can have their cake and eat it to.

The key with symptoms is not why, why is this symptom here, or what type of symptom is it, but simply to notice what the message is that the innate wisdom of your body is telling you. LISTEN to what it says, and take action. I will get to how and what this innate wisdom is, says and does. Promise. If you know when your inner wisdom talks to you, and what it says, great. Begin listening now.

In case you really want to know which symptoms are which, I will tell you how to know. You just know. It is NOT something you can figure out with your mind. It goes deeper than that, to a knowing.

It is your inner knowing that knows 100% about what is happening, what symptoms are which and what they mean. This inner knowing is what some others might refer to as the heart brain, or their instinct, or gut feeling.

Joseph Chilton Pierce summed it up best in his book, *Biology of Transcendence*, in that he showed how physically, neurologically, the human brain has formed a fourth part, the Heart Brain. There is the reptilian brain, the limbic brain, the cortex, and the heart brain, which is what I am calling your Inner Knowing. This is the part of you that has access to all the intellectual knowing, plus that other 99.9% that we do not know about. This Inner Knowing goes beyond the wisdom of the body. And it is this Inner Knowing that knows, exactly, every time, what to do. It is just that mostly we don't act on the knowing, or should I say wisdom, it gives us.

Let me give you an example. Have you ever been at a family dinner, or somewhere where the food was so good, and you were so full that you even said to yourself, "I am so full, I should stop eating"? And you continued to eat anyway?

Or how about being up late at night, watching a movie or doing some work or something, and then you say to yourself, or maybe even out loud, "I am tired, I should go to bed." But then you don't because there are only fourteen minutes left in the movie, or there is only a little more work to do, and you want to finish.

This is the inner knowing I am talking about. It knows what is best for us, all the time, and even tells us, yet we often don't listen.

This inner knowing goes beyond the intellect, to a wisdom that is far greater than what we know consciously. It knows what type of symptom you are expressing. And, frankly, it doesn't care. Because it knows what is important is the message it is giving you—the message not to eat that anymore, or do that, or whatever. And we know. We just don't listen.

If you are still wondering how you can know what this inner wisdom is telling you, I will address that in more detail in a later chapter.

What is important for this chapter is that the innate wisdom is constantly giving you "symptoms" to listen to, to act on to help yourself heal. Symptoms are communication from the innate wisdom trying to get what it wants. Sometimes it is telling you to do something, or not do something. Sometimes it is just telling you to improve your health. There is a message within that symptom. You do not have to know what the symptom is or even what the cause of the symptom is in order to heal.

All you have to know is what the symptoms are telling you to do or not do. It is usually just a matter of listening or not, of knowing that these are just messages from your body to get you to do something, something that adds to your health, so that your body can heal itself the way it was designed to.

Chapter 8

What You Don't Know Can Hurt You. . . in Fact, Kill You

There is a big distinction I will emphasize again. It is the difference between emergency medical care, and medical symptom and disease care. Emergency medical care is exactly that, the type of care you would get if you cut yourself, had an accident, slipped and fell, etc. Something happened, you are hurt, and you get medical care. Medical symptom and disease care is also exactly that, the part of medicine that deals with *trying*—and I emphasize trying—to help people heal their symptoms and disease.

Emergency medical care is great. They are wonderful at saving lives during times of crisis. No one does it better. The problem is that the medical symptoms and disease care system has been lumped together with emergency medical care. When someone makes a negative comment about doctors, immediately people get defensive because they also think of emergency medical care. And everyone knows the emergency medical care system saves lives. Many people know someone who has directly been saved by the emergency medical care system.

I am sure that the medical symptoms and disease care system has also saved some lives. The time has now come to put the medical symptoms and disease care system in its proper place. And this can be done without changing emergency medical care. Emergency medical care can remain right where it is.

Unfortunately, I have been unable to find any place that sees medicine as these two separate parts, at least when it comes to statistics, studies, measures, and anything concrete. So I will talk about things that the medical system states. Mainly this information refers to the medical symptoms and disease care system.

Everyone knows that emergency medical care saves lives, probably hundreds of thousands, if not millions of lives, each year in the US alone. This I also know. I see the emergency medical care system as an essential part of health care. It is great, and it is making huge improvements in saving peoples lives.

The medical symptom and disease care system, on the other hand, is the system I will be referring to any time I talk about medicine. And here is how what you don't know might kill you.

The American Medical Association (AMA) admitted that the medical system was the third leading cause of death in the US, second only to heart disease and cancer. They used their own studies and published it in their own journal, the *Journal of the American Medical Association*, in the July 26th 2000 issue. They themselves said that they were the third leading cause of death. There is no study, no statistics, nothing to manipulate or play with. They, the AMA, said this themselves.

I know as well as everyone else, that you can prove anything with statistics, like the studies, funded by tobacco companies, that proved smoking was safe, etc. We all know the tobacco companies have a vested interest in showing that smoking is safe.

If the tobacco companies did studies that actually showed that smoking is not safe, it would be a good bet to believe them. When the tobacco companies finally admit, themselves, that smoking is bad for you, you kind of have to believe them, because that is not the result they want. In fact, it is just the opposite.

Now, let me ask you: Do you think the medical system wants to admit to a low number of people they kill each year, or a high one? Obviously, they do not want to kill any people. Most doctors on an individual level truly want to help people, truly want to do what is best for their patients. They do not want to harm them, cause injury, or kill them, I promise you. So when the medical system admitted that they were the third leading cause of death in the US, even though this is not something they wanted to admit to, like the tobacco companies, and since the medical system used their own studies, and said it themselves, you kind of have to believe them.

Yes, friends, the medical establishment themselves said they were the third leading cause of death in the US.

Disbelief is the first reaction that people have here. They don't want to believe this.

If they really said this, how come you have not heard about it until now? Well, let me ask you: If you'd just killed 225,000 people, would you be out telling everyone? Would you be out putting it on the front page of newspapers? Or would you try to hide the fact and bury it?

You don't have to believe me. Just look in the July 26th 2000 issue of the *Journal of American Medical Association*. You can read them admit to this, and see it for yourself. But in case you don't want to do that, I will put the same thing they said in the following pages.

This will raise some fears for people. It is fearful to think that some group can kill 225,000 Americans every year and get away with it, year after year after year.

There are some who will accuse me of doing exactly what the medical profession does, using fear to control people to do a certain thing.

What I am doing is giving you the information and facts. If you want to make an educated choice, instead of guessing and operating from ignorance or opinions or responding out of fear, you have to be educated by having the information and facts. And that is what this chapter is about. It is just that much of this information and these facts are *scary*.

On top of the 225,000 people the medical system kills each year, there is more. There are unnecessary procedures, unwanted negative effects, extra visits, extra medications, more hospital admissions, and billions of extra dollars for all the errors that do not end in someone dying.

If this is confrontational, if you don't want to believe this, neither do I. You must face that it is published referenced facts by the AMA themselves. In fact the very people I am talking about published these facts. If these are confronting, and you don't want to believe them, there are a couple of common reasons that I have found for this.

The biggest reason is that emergency medical care (EMC) saves lives. The lines are blurred between the EMC and medical symptoms and disease care.

You want to believe that someone else out there is looking after your best interests…the government, someone, anyone. You don't want to believe that money and corruption could go on that long and kill that many people. With things that bad, why would the government or anyone else not stop it, or expose it?

Another common reason goes back to one of the benefits of not being healthy. You get to avoid responsibility. And if the above were true, which it is, then you would have no one else to make responsible for your health, you would be forced to be in charge of your own health. Many people do not like this.

All I am saying right now is that this is what the medical system has admitted to themselves. It is very scary that it has gotten this bad, and yet no one has done anything about it yet. I want to answer the question of why. Why has no one done anything about it? For one simple reason…the American Medical Association.

See, medicine is a touchy subject. They have the courts and laws on their side right now. Let me give you some examples.

If someone came to me and wanted me to naturally help them heal, and they died, I would probably lose my license and be fined. If someone went to the medical profession and they were treated, and they died, that would just be a person that could not be helped. And nothing would happen to the medical professional.

If I recommend something for you to treat your symptoms or disease and it doesn't work, I am responsible. But if you do what the medical symptoms and disease care system wants you to do and it doesn't work, you are responsible. They are not. Isn't that interesting?

The medical symptoms and disease care system has a magical veil of protection. And it is time to get rid of the veil of protection, because they are killing 225,000 people a year with the license to kill given to them by the laws and courts.

If I told you to take X to cure your cancer, the AMA could, and probably would, sue me, especially if I got many people to take X. Even if a medical doctor did the same thing, they would probably sue him. And if someone took X and ended up dying, their family would sue me or the medical doctor for sure, and win. Why?

Medicine has the home field advantage. The laws state that you cannot do anything that is not reasonable and customary and is not proven to be more effective than medicine. Now, what is reasonable and customary? Everything the medical profession currently does. And this is where the catch lies. You cannot perform some form of treatment unless it is proven. But how can you prove it if you cannot do it? Exactly. That is why the same treatments for cancer that were used in the 1960s—chemotherapy, radiation, and surgery—are still being done today.

It is not exactly true that you cannot perform a treatment unless it is proven. You can get money, grants, and special permission, and then do a controlled clinical trial, etc., etc. And, guess what the price tag of all this is? At minimum, $100 million. Then you will not get X approved due to one study; you must do more studies. Pretty much only the drug companies can come up with that kind of money and resources to make it happen. Or you can get funding from the government, but the government only gives out $5.4 million a year to study natural health care. That is not even enough for one-tenth of a single study. That is one reason why the medical system still maintains control and still has its magical veil of protection.

So if you told someone to take X for their cancer and you were licensed, no matter what your license is, you could have your license taken away from you. If the person ended up dying, whether or not you were licensed, you could be sued and the punishment could include fines and jail time.

But, if the medical system does chemotherapy, radiation, and surgery and the person ends up dying anyway, there were no laws broken, and nothing out of the reasonable and customary was done. So everything is fine.

This is how the medical symptoms and disease care system has been able to maintain their monopoly for so long, how they have the courts and laws on their side. And this is true in all areas that the medical symptoms and disease care system has their hand in. They get the benefit of the doubt even if their ideas and theories are less tested and validated than someone else's.

As a non medical and symptoms disease care practitioner, not only do you have to do studies, you have to do them their way, the $100 million way. And often they do not have to do any studies, because they automatically get the benefit of the doubt. They make what "reasonable and customary" is. I will talk more about this in the next chapter.

How have they been able to hide the fact that they kill 225,000 people per year? Because they have the money, laws, and courts on their side.

The information and statistics on the following pages were published in the July 26th 2000 issue of the *Journal of the American Medical Association*, one of the most prestigious and well respected medical journals in the world. Said another way, when something is in there, the medical symptoms and disease care system has given it their endorsement.

All of this is what the medical symptom and disease care system has admitted to. I am going strictly with what the medical profession has directly admitted to, with no doctoring, no additions, NOTHING, simply restating what they have said.

The number of people the medical system kills each year:

- Unnecessary surgery: 12,000
- Medication errors in hospitals: 7,000
- Other errors in hospitals: 20,000
- Infections in hospitals: 80,000

- Non-error, negative effects of drugs (drugs given correctly, taken correctly, but the unknown side effect was death!): 106,000

These add up to 225,000 deaths per year from iatrogenic causes!

What does the word "iatrogenic" mean? The word means "induced," and this term has become defined as induced in a patient by a physician's activity, manner, or therapy; it is used especially for a complication of treatment.

Said another way, 225,000 people are killed by doctors and hospitals and what they do! These 225,000 deaths per year makes the medical system the third leading cause of death in the United States, after deaths from heart disease and cancer.

Between 4% and 18% of the time people go to the hospital and are not killed, they experience things like this;

- 116 million extra physician visits
- 77 million extra prescriptions
- 17 million emergency department visits
- 8 million hospitalizations
- 3 million long-term admissions
- 199,000 additional deaths
- $77 billion in extra costs

We put up with these numbers because we think of these outcomes as a "casualty of war," that these numbers are necessary for all the good that medicine does and for all the lives it supposedly saves; these outcomes are part of saving lives and making our health in America better.

This would be great, if that were actually true. If the medical symptoms and disease care system actually saved lives and produced better health for us. But do they?

Of 13 countries in a recent comparison, the United States ranks an average of 12th or almost the worst. This statistic was also published in the same article of JAMA.

Here are the actual numbers the medical system admitted to:

- 13th (last) for low-birth-weight percentages
- 13th for neonatal mortality and infant mortality overall
- 11th for post-neonatal mortality

- 13th for years of potential life lost (excluding external causes)
- 11th for life expectancy at one year for females, 12th for males
- 10th for life expectancy at 15 years for females, 12th for males
- 10th for life expectancy at 40 years for females, 9th for males
- 7th for life expectancy at 65 years for females, 7th for males
- 3rd for life expectancy at 80 years for females, 3rd for males
- 10th for age-adjusted mortality

The World Health Organization confirms this as well. They used data from more countries and ranked the United States as 15th among 25 industrialized countries.

There is a perception that the American public "behaves badly" by smoking, drinking and being violent. But if you look at the facts, it just isn't true.

This is the ranking of the same 13 countries above, where we were second to last in health care results:

- Females who smoke ranges from 14% in Japan to 41% in Denmark; in the United States, it is 24%, the fifth best
- For males, the range is from 26% in Sweden to 61% in Japan; it is 28% in the United States, the third best
- The US ranks fifth best for alcoholic beverage consumption
- The US has relatively low consumption of animal fats (fifth lowest in men aged 55-64 years in 20 industrialized countries) and the third lowest average cholesterol concentrations among men aged 50 to 70 years

Even though we spend more money per capita on health care than every other country except Germany, and we have healthier lifestyles than people in most other countries, we still rank almost last with regards to our actual level of health.

Our medical system kills 225,000 people per year, and we still have almost the worst health of any industrialized nation. This goes to show the medical system does not give us health. Because they attempt to treat symptoms and disease does not mean that leaves you with health.

The number of deaths that the AMA said happens, 225,000 each year, are not worth the results we are getting for our health.

Now, I want to put this into a slightly different perspective. I did some research, because I wanted to know. Depending on whose numbers you use, there are about 600 million to 1.2 billion people per year traveling on airplanes in the US alone. There are about 600 million to 900 million visits to a medical doctor each year in the US.

Let's say that roughly the same number of people step onto a plane as step into a doctors' office. A jumbo jet holds roughly 250-300 passengers, depending on the airline and how full it is. If the airline industry was killing 225,000 people every year, it would be the equivalent of 1,000 jumbo jets worth of people (225,000 people divided by 225 passengers total) dying every year, if you divide 1,000 planes worth of people by 365 days in the year.

Comparing the two (it is uncanny how well the numbers work out) and you get two jumbo jets crashing every DAY, with everyone on board being killed.

Imagine if you wake up tomorrow and all over the news you see: "Two Jumbo Jets Crashed, and Everyone on Board Is Killed!" Then the next day: "Two jumbo jets crashed today, and everyone is dead." Then the next day: "Two jumbo jets crashed again today, and everyone was killed…" The next day: "Two more jumbo jets crashed today, no survivors, everyone dead…" The next day: "Two jumbo jets crashed today, and all passengers were killed, everyone dead." You think to yourself that you are supposed to go on a flight next week. Do you cancel? Then the next day, again, two jumbo jets crash, killing everyone on board. The next day, two jumbo jets crash, no survivors. When is it you decide to not fly? How many days does it take of two jumbo jets crashing every day before you decide not to fly? How long before you start talking to your family about not flying? How long before you decide it is worth your time to do what it takes to be well?

The next day, two more jumbo jets crash and burn, and everyone on board is killed. It has only been eight days.

I want you to pause and think here for a moment. Do this for real. I want you to imagine what would it really be like if, every day, two jumbo jets crashed, killing everyone on board, leaving no survivors. How long before the airline industry would be out of business? How long before the government would step in and do something? What would the news media be like? What would people be saying and talking about?

Now, the reality is a little different, because air travel is mostly for convenience. Supposedly doctors are saving peoples lives, and the emergency medical care system is. The medical symptoms and disease care system isn't. That is why I make the distinction between the emergency medical care system and medical symptoms and disease care. Medical symptoms and disease care does not save tons of lives, does not prolong masses of people's lives, does not make the quality of life better for most people. I can even show you that they do not save more lives than they kill.

If the doctors quit working, and they saved more lives then the number of people they killed, the death rate should go up, right? If doctors help more people then they kill, more people should die if doctors quit working. That is common sense. And if doctors quit working, and the death rate went down, that would mean they are killing more people then they are saving. I mean, if fewer people died, and there were fewer doctors working, that would mean, overall, that they helped fewer people than they hurt. Because if they helped more people, when they quit working, the death rate would go up.

But how can you test this theory out? How can you get doctors to quit working? Well, have them go on strike. There are many countries around the world where the doctors have gone on strike. And, interestingly enough, you know what happened? The death rate went down. Yes, down. Fewer people died when there were fewer visits to doctors. This would imply that doctors actually hurt more people than they help.

In Israel, this is exactly what happened. The doctors went on strike, and the death rates went down "considerably," according to the *British Medical Journal* (*BMJ* 2000;320:1561: 10 June). Also, in the book, *Confessions of a Medical Heretic*, Robert S. Mendelsohn, M.D. wrote:

> In 1976 in Bogota, Colombia, doctors went on strike during a 52-day period. The death rate went down 35% during that time. In Los Angeles in 1976, doctors went on strike to protest the increasing costs of malpractice insurance. The death rate decreased

by 18%. When the strike ended, the death rate returned to pre-strike proportions. In Israel in 1973, during a month-long strike, the death rate dropped 50%. The last time the death rate had been that low was when there was a doctors' strike 20 years before.

Doctors go on strike, and the death rate goes down, over and over again. This seems like a pretty good indicator that doctors hurt more people than they help. I will show you how true this really is, with more later.

I want to remind you here again that I make a distinction between emergency medical care, and medical symptom and disease care. Medical symptom and disease care is what I am referring to with this information.

I want to go back to the tobacco companies for a moment, to point out something else here. If the tobacco companies will admit that smoking causes X-amount of damage, what do you think the real amount of damage is? A lot more, that is for sure. They do not want to admit that smoking causes a lot of problems. If they did, they would be liable for a lot more money.

The medical system admits to killing 225,000 people per year. What do you think the actual number is? What is the real number, more or less? If this is what they admitted to, I definitely think it is more.

How these statistics are tracked is that everything gets a code. For every diagnosis, there is a standard code that everyone goes by. For every surgery and treatment, there is a standard code that all doctors use for the same thing. For most deaths, there is a code. Everything in medicine is standardized in this way. When people die, it is up to the medical doctor, to give an appropriate code for why they died. That is how we know that X-number of people died in car crashes, or from drug overdose, or from heart attacks, or from cancer. They all have separate codes. Then the medical system just adds them up.

Let's say someone was given a medication and it caused their liver to fail, and they died. There is a different code for liver failure, than there is for medication error causing liver failure, than there is for doctor error.

The person is dead because their liver failed, and there is nothing that can be done to bring them back. Nothing. Now the doctor has to put down the cause of death.

Imagine yourself in the doctor's shoes. You screwed up, a person is dead, and if it is really your fault, you might get sued, and lose your license. What code would you be tempted to put down? Liver failure due to medication error? Or that it was your fault? The person is dead. Nothing can be done to bring them back. You can learn from your mistakes either way. What do you choose?

What if the case is borderline? Did you screw up or not? It is a grey area. You followed standard protocol, and there was something that, had you known, you could have prevented the person's death. But you didn't know. And there was no reason why you should have known, because standard protocol did not pick up on it. What code do you put down? Liver failure from medication error, or your fault?

Or even greyer, the patient had a weak liver. You know this, and they knew the medication might cause liver failure, but the patient didn't want to change, and wanted to take the medication. The patient's liver failed and they died. What do you put down for the code? Liver failure? Or liver failure due to medication error?

Now, many errors don't even have codes for them. Even if the doctor wanted to report the real cause of death, he couldn't. Because the medical symptoms and disease care system has not created codes for all the ways the system can kill you.

Again, these are the numbers the medical system admitted that they had caused. I wish I had a clue what the real numbers were. I don't. But I can promise you one thing, they are higher.

The emergency medical care system is EXCELLENT at helping people who have been in accidents. If I needed emergency care, you can bet your life that you would see me at the ER of a hospital.

This is where, undoubtedly, they save lives. The unfortunate part is that, so far, the two systems have not been separated. They do not separate accident- and trauma-related care from medical symptoms and disease care when reporting statistics. They are all grouped into the same category.

The rest of this chapter is my opinion. I have not done all the research (finding all the sources, and adding up all the numbers, etc., as it would be a lot) and I will give my opinion on the information I do have. Starting right now, the following section is my opinion only, based on logic and what seems to me to be common sense.

I was able to find statistics on individual hospitals, and it seems that 20%-50% of their admissions were due to trauma. The difference I noticed seemed to be that some hospitals specialized in trauma where others did not. It is a total guess, but logic would say that the percentage of traumatic outpatient visits would be less. So 20% would be the number I come up with as to how many doctor visits are trauma related.

Let's assume that the error rate is about the same as well. This would mean that approximately 20% would be the numbers reported for people they killed, in my opinion, for the number of useless deaths. This would bring the overall number of people the medical symptoms and disease care establishment kills each year to about 200,000 people, but the percentage, when compared with plane crashes, would remain the same because we would also subtract the number of visits for trauma care when coming up with the figures.

That being said, maybe trauma care kills a higher percentage of people, or maybe there is a higher percentage of outpatient trauma visits. Even if we take the best case scenario for arguing the medical symptoms and disease care side, here is where we come up with:

Let's say 50% of all visits to the medical profession are trauma related, and medical personnel actually make twice as many errors in trauma care as they do during regular visits for symptom and disease care. This would put the number of people needlessly killed by medical symptoms and disease care at 75,000 each year.

Again, doing the math means that 75,000 people are killed by the medical profession in non-trauma related situations. Those 75,000 people's comprising half of the visits still leaves one jumbo jet crashing every day. Every day, another jumbo jet crashes. Next day, one jumbo jet crashes, and everyone on board is killed. Next day, one jumbo jet crashes, everyone on board is killed. And on and on. Day after day, week after week, month after month, year after year, one jumbo jet crashes every day, killing everyone on board needlessly.

Apart from emergency care, medicine does NOTHING, absolutely nothing to help people improve their health. It only treat symptoms and disease. It does nothing to help people prevent sickness, symptoms and disease. And, in my opinion, it is actually counter-productive to increasing health and preventing disease. So these 75,000 deaths are at the cost of no gain, nothing. Completely senseless deaths. When it comes to health, the medical profession does nothing to help people heal. I will get into why a little later, in a factual way, so that you will understand this for yourself as well.

For now, my major point with this chapter is to wake you up to the reality of the medical profession, sharing information with you so that you can make a more informed choice about who will do something about your health.

And in case you missed it, you are the person who has to do something about your health. The medical profession is not going to create a magic pill or potion or lotion that will magically give you health. You will either add to your health, or lose your health. It is that simple.

Insanity is doing the same thing over and over and expecting a different result. The medical symptoms and disease care system has been trying to treat symptoms and disease for almost 100 years, with no real results. They still have essentially no cures or treatments for most things. The very fact that 1.25 million people die every year in America from heart disease and cancer alone is proof of that, not to mention all the other thousands of diseases that people still die from.

The medical symptoms and disease care system has made no real progress in curing symptoms or disease.

Chapter 9

Modern Medicine Is Not Scientific

Modern medicine is *NOT* scientific.

This is a pretty bold claim, because most doctors and people take it as fact that medicine is very scientific.

Again, I am picking on the medical symptoms and disease care approach. Emergency medicine is great. They are actually scientific. I really want to make clear here again the difference between emergency care, and symptoms and disease care. Modern medicine and its disease and symptom treatment gets a halo because emergency care people save lives. The two totally different, and completely separate, sides of medicine do things completely different.

To show you how medicine is the farthest thing from scientific, I have to first share with you what "scientific" means. But don't worry. As I promised in the beginning, this will be fun, unlike most science classes you probably took, unless you had a good teacher.

I am showing you how medicine is non-scientific, because that is their biggest argument about how medicine works and how great it is, and how natural health care doesn't work. How their supposedly being scientific is in part where they get this magical veil of protection they currently have.

In showing you this, I will also prove that natural health care is actually more scientific than medicine. Using medicine's own proof, I will prove that natural health care actually works better and is more scientific than medicine.

How science works is like this:

1. Science develops a hypothesis (a fancy word for an educated guess about how something works) based on current ways of thinking
2. Scientists attempt to prove or disprove the hypothesis. They do this by setting up tests, and creating new ways to best measure the test and if it worked or not
3. If the hypothesis is proved wrong once, science looks for a new hypothesis.

Scientists may use the current hypothesis until they find a better one, but science knows it is not true and has flaws. That is essentially how science works.

Medicine, on the other hand, doesn't use that method. What They do is this:

1. They develop a hypothesis based on old ways of thinking
2. They accept the hypothesis as true, until the majority proves it wrong. And the majority can be hundreds, if not thousands of times versus the one-time proof of science
3. When things are finally proven wrong by the majority, often 70 years or more later, they finally change their theory a bit so it is not so wrong.
4. They expect everyone else to prove a new hypothesis by using medicine's measurement tools which worked best for medicine previously.

Let's start at the beginning:

Coming up with theories based on current ways of thinking.
Medicine comes up with theories based on old ways of thinking.

Modern medicine still views the human body as a machine. They still see the body as a bunch of separate, independent systems, and believe that if you can find out enough information about the individual parts, then you can understand the whole. If they can just figure out how to fix the parts, then they will be able to help people heal.

This is called Newtonian physics, where the sum of the parts can be broken down and studied to understand the whole. It works great with clocks and machines, but not so well with humans, because a human is more than a machine with no internal intelligence.

Through the early 1900s, in science, Newtonian physics was slowly being replaced by quantum physics. And, in 1927, it was pretty much complete. Quantum physics was the new understanding in the science of the future.

The basic principle of quantum physics is very easy: The whole is MORE than the sum of the parts. $1+1$ = more than 2. This is essentially what quantum physics says.

This is the idea of wholistic (yes, with a w) health care, working with the person as a whole, and not just the parts, because the whole is more than the parts. On point number 1, natural health care is actually more scientific than medicine. Natural health care recognizes that there is an innate wisdom that runs and controls things, and that this inner wisdom knows more than all the doctors on the planet put together. The medical symptoms and disease care system still views the body as a machine that needs to be fixed, that is not capable of healing itself.

But did medicine did change its theories in 1927 to reflect this new understanding? Nope, in fact, they still have not really changed their views today. They still look at the parts of the body and try to figure out how to make the parts better, thinking they will then make the whole better. (Picture me shaking my head like a parent whose kid still has not learned from the same mistake they have been making over and over and over and over again.)

When they come up with new ideas and theories about ways to help people, it is almost always based on Newtonian physics, physics that was proven wrong over 70 years ago. And anything that was based on Newtonian physics is also wrong, according to science.

For over 70 years, the AMA has been holding onto the theory that the body is a machine, and refusing to change their theory. And yet, most people know that the body is more than a machine. It has more to it then just the parts that make it up. Maybe soon this will be embraced, because the evidence is starting to get overwhelming, even for the AMA.

Accepting that the hypothesis as true until the majority proves it wrong.

Medicine holds onto its theories tooth and nail. It fights for them until the very last minute. Why, I am not really sure, but it doesn't matter why; they just do. See the above paragraph, which shows how they refuse to change, not only the first time their theory is proven wrong, but 70 years after it was proven wrong. They still refuse to accept the new reality.

Even when there are hundreds of cases in which their theory has been proven wrong, they still say things like: "Yeah, but those are the exceptions, those are just flukes, those are not true, that cannot happen."

The medical symptoms and disease care system has been doing the same thing to treat cancer for over 30 years, and still nothing is different. There are many treatments that have a better cure rate than chemo, radiation and/or surgery, yet the medical system holds on. This is another great example of how they refuse to change, how they want to hold onto their ideas and theories, how they want to hold on until the evidence becomes so overwhelming that they have to change. This is beginning to happen. People are finally waking up to the fact there are much better ways than radiation, surgery, and chemotherapy to help people with cancer, better than the same thing that hasn't worked. More about cancer later.

Let me give you a couple more examples: vitamins, cholesterol, spinal cord injuries, removing tonsils and appendixes. For years, medicine emphatically stated that vitamins were a waste of money; you were just getting expensive urine. Vitamins did nothing, they insisted. The studies grew. The evidence mounted. They held onto their theory that vitamins are useless. The evidence kept coming in, kept coming in, and despite the overwhelming evidence that vitamins actually did make a difference, they still denied that vitamins were of any benefit. Then, in recent years, they finally had no choice, because if they still tried to stand behind their position that vitamins were of no use, everyone would have seen them for the idiots they were, because vitamins are beneficial for peoples' health and well being.

Spinal cord injuries: For years the medical profession said nerves do not regenerate. It was impossible. Once you had nerve damage, that was it. Yet there are numerous cases of people healing from spinal cord injuries. For the longest time, doctors said that was impossible, that cannot happen. As the cases came in, they looked the other way, pretended they did not exist, instead of looking at how people were doing it so that they could possibly help others; they fought for their theory that nerves cannot and do not regenerate.

Tonsils: Doctors used to do a "two for one sale" on removing tonsils. If one kid was scheduled to have his/her tonsils out, they'd say bring in your other kid and we will do them for free to help prevent future problems. Now they don't do that, because they realized after years of mounting evidence, that tonsils help keep people from getting upper respiratory infections. They also realized that when people had their tonsils out, they were more likely to get infections in their lungs, the place the infection went once the tonsils were gone. They realized that the tonsils were like gatekeepers. They kept the bacteria from going into the lungs. The tonsils kept the bacteria in the tonsils. Rather than looking at why the body was not able to take care of the bacteria, doctors just removed the tonsils, because that was what they thought was the one cause and one cure. For me, I would much rather have a sore throat than a lung infection any day.

The same with the appendix. The doctors decided to take out people's appendixes left and right if it even seemed the appendix might only be inflamed. They knew the appendix didn't really do anything anyway. Then, as the evidence started pouring in, they finally gave up their theory that the appendix does nothing. They found the appendix actually helps fight bacteria. They found that when you take out the appendix, people were more likely to get colon cancer.

For years, the medical profession said that eating cholesterol made your cholesterol levels high. And finally, under overwhelming evidence, they are slowly changing their theory. They are recognizing it is not the eating of cholesterol that makes your levels high, but the eating of sugar and refined products that makes your cholesterol high. They are realizing that when people quit eating carbs and refined products like sugar and flour, their cholesterol levels went down, within weeks, almost every time. Even though their idea was just a theory, and all the evidence that has ever been done proved the exact opposite, they still held on.

I could go on and on, but I think you are getting the picture. The medical profession wants to hold on to their theories and be right, rather than throw out the old theory and get a new one, the way science does. Or at least use it, until a better new one comes along, while knowing, the old theory was not true. If they did this it would actually allow the medical symptoms and disease care system to be open to new ideas, like science. But they don't, they hold on to their theories until they have to change them.

Finally change only after 70 years and overwhelming evidence.

Science changes right away when something is proven wrong only once. If it is proven wrong once, it is wrong. Period. Science knows this, yet medicine does not seem to grasp that idea. For over 70 years, the medical field has been holding on to their Newtonian-based practices. And since Newtonian physics was proven wrong, anything that is based on it is also wrong. Medicine is not a science. It is ideas based on theories that are wrong. If the ideas it is based on are wrong, how can medicine be right?

Let me say this another way. Let's say you have a theory that gravity pushes rocks away from the earth. You get a bunch of rocks, attach them all over to a box, and if you are in the box, you will float up in the air. Now, since the first theory, "gravity pushes rocks up" is wrong, your following idea, that a box with rocks all over it will be pushed away by gravity, is also wrong.

Science knows this, yet medicine refuses to accept this fact. They continue to base their ideas on theories that were proven wrong over 70 years ago.

Proving with the same measuring tool.

This one is my favorite. I'll tell you a story.

There is a guy whom we will call Jack. Jack invents a machine that can change how comfortable it is to be in a room in your house. It is called a heater. This heater makes the room more comfortable to be in, especially during winter. Now, Jack wants to measure how well his machine works, because there are other people claiming their machine works better. So Jack must invent a tool to measure how well his machine works. He invents a thermometer. He measures the room before he puts his heater in the room, and then after, and the thermometer proves that his machine made the room more comfortable. The thermometer can also show how much better his heater is at increasing the temperature of the room, thus proving how well it works against all other heaters. His measuring device is great at doing this.

Then there is Jane. She also invents something that makes the room more comfortable to sit in. It is called a big reclining chair. Now, Jack invented his machine to make the room more comfortable to be in. Jack doesn't like this competition, so he sets out to prove that Jane's device doesn't work. He uses his measuring tool, because it worked in the past. He measures the room before the big reclining chair is in the room. Jack then puts the big reclining chair in the room, puts his thermometer on the chair, and nothing happens. His thermometer does not change. So he goes around saying, "See? With my measuring tool I proved your machine does not make the room more comfortable."

Now, this is a funny little story, because if you have not guessed, it is exactly what the medical profession has done. They invented something they said was health care, but actually it is symptoms and disease care. And they used medicine to treat symptoms and disease. They invented a study to test how well these medicines worked. It was called a double-blind study. They then expect that no matter how people help improve other people's health, they must use "their" measuring tool, to see how well the new thing works.

There are more ways to make a room comfortable than by changing the temperature. There are also more ways to heal people who have symptoms than by treating them with medications. If you have a different theory, you need a different measuring tool. You need an appropriate measuring tool to test your new way of doing things, or a different way of doing things. Science knows this, yet medicine is saying their way, the double-blind study, is the only way to measure whether a person is healthier or not.

Wholistic care uses different ways, based on quantum physics, to help people heal, not Newtonian Physics like medicine uses. If you are testing new theories, you need new ways of measuring them. The old ways of measuring do not work any more. Imagine trying to test modern breakthroughs in science with equipment from the 1800s. That is what medicine is asking people to do—use this machine from 1890 to see if what you have today works.

Just as the comfort level of a room is more than heat, health care is more than treating symptoms and disease with medication and surgery. Medicine is not health care. It is symptoms and disease care. And if you do anything other than symptoms and disease care with medicine, you need a different way to measure what you do.

Yet medicine thinks everyone should use their measuring tool, because it worked best for them.

To review: Medicine bases theories on 70-year-old ideas that are wrong. Medicine maintains a theory until it is proven wrong by the majority, and expects to use the same measuring tool for everything, because it worked well in one situation.

Natural health care develops a theory based on modern, proven theories. The theory is thrown out if it doesn't work, or at least used with the full knowledge that it is not true until something better comes along.

The most accurate measuring tool is used to see how well the theory works.

That sure seems a lot more scientific than medicine. What medicine is really saying, when they shout "scientific" is, Did you do exactly what we did? Did you do things like us? Well, I do NOT want to do things the way they are doing them. Look at the results they are getting. Look at the level of health in America. I do not want to do the same things they do, because look what it has gotten us. My favorite definition of insanity is doing the same thing over and over and expecting a different result. Treating people over and over again with the same old theories and ways of doing things, and expecting a different result. Expecting people to finally get healthy. It just isn't working.

One more thing that is really interesting to me. Medical practitioners, when they are approached with anything that is not accepted by what medicine is all about, demand to know: Where is your proof? Where is your study? Is it scientific?

Well, let me ask them the same question. Please, show me the double-blind studies for surgery, all the surgeries you do that are not trauma related. Show me the studies that prove their effectiveness. Please do. This is a challenge. I am asking the so-called scientific medical community where are all their studies on surgery. Where are all their studies like the ones they want everyone else to have? Where are their studies on the effectiveness of surgery? Please, send them to me.

I have actually seen a couple of double-blind studies on surgery, and every one actually proved that NOT doing the surgery was either MORE effective or just as effective as actually doing the surgery. Yes, cutting people and putting the marks on the outside as if they had done the actual surgery, was just as effective as actually doing the surgery.

This is what I was talking about earlier, how they often do not even have to do the same studies they require of everyone else. They automatically get the reasonable and customary, without even doing the same studies they want everyone else to do. It is time to make natural health care the reasonable and customary, and make the medical symptoms and disease care system prove that they are more effective and safer than natural methods. I mean, after all, natural health care has just as many studies as they do.

Actually, natural health care has more studies that prove how effective it is. They are case studies. The best measurement tool for how natural health care adds health back into the body is case studies. And natural health care has tons and tons of case studies. That is also why natural health care is actually more validated than many things the medical symptoms and disease care system uses. It is just not validated with the faulty measuring tool of a $100 million double-blind study.

What is interesting to me is that every time I pose this challenge to a traditional medical doctor, I always hear something like, "Well, you cannot use double-blind studies for surgery." Or "You can just look at the person and know the surgery worked." Or "You just ask the person how they are doing after surgery to know if the surgery worked." Or "If they didn't die, the surgery worked."

There are some studies, case studies, of how surgery works. And these seem to be good enough for surgery, but not for other techniques or ways of healing.

And I always wonder, for something like surgery, why is it OK not to use a double-blind study, but everyone else in the world must prove what they have with a double-blind study? Does this make sense to you?

With different ways of doing things, and doing different things, you need different ways of measuring the results. Science gets this, and maybe one day medicine will as well.

I'll tell you another story. It is about my dad. My dad had a watch given to him for a present after retiring from his job. And this watch was the best. It kept perfect time. Day in and day out, year after year, this watch kept perfect time. Decades passed, and the watch still kept perfect time. Then, the watch began to slow down. It did not keep perfect time anymore.

So my dad asked around, talked to all his friends, and found the best watch repairman in the state. The person whom everyone said was the very best.

My dad brought his watch to the watch repairman, and the watch repairman took a look at his watch. He listened to it, felt it, ran all the tests he knew how to run on the watch, and came up with the solution.

The watch repairman told my dad he had figured out the problem. The problem with his watch was that there was an extra piece the manufacturer of the watch had put into the watch. This piece was not really that necessary. If the watch repairman took this piece out, the watch would work like new again.

If you are like my dad, you are probably thinking right now: That is stupid. The watch worked just fine, and now, when you take out an "extra piece" the watch will work again like new? Crazy. And that is what my dad thought, so he took his watch somewhere else. He took it to another watch repairman. This one specializing in watches that lose time.

My dad thought it was quite interesting, and didn't even know there was a watch specialist who specialized in watches that lose time. It seemed kind of interesting, because how many things could cause the watch to lose time? my dad wondered. It could be many things, but the watch repairman was the specialist, so my dad took the watch in to the specialist.

And after a while, this specialist said the same thing. There was an extra piece in the watch, and once it was removed, the watch would run like new again. My dad would have to set it every once in a while, but that is it. Hmm, my dad thought. Two people told him the same thing, so that must be the problem, even though it made absolutely no sense to him whatsoever. So he agreed to let the specialist take out the extra piece.

When my dad got his watch back, it still didn't work right. In fact, it didn't tell time at all anymore. And when my dad asked the watch repair person about this, the watch repair person said: Oh yeah, after we take out that extra piece, you have to set your watch to the correct time, every time you want to know what time it is, so you can know what time it is.

My dad said, What? You are telling me that I have to look at a clock, set my watch to that other clock that works, and then look at my watch to tell what time it is? Is that what you meant by set the watch every once in a while? And the watch repairer said Yes. But look how much easier it is to set the time now, with that piece gone.

This story really isn't about my dad. I made it up. I made it up because you are probably saying: That is so stupid. He should have known the problem was not an extra piece that needed to be taken out. It worked just fine for years, and then suddenly, the "extra piece" was causing the problems, and taking it out would fix the problem? How ridiculous. I agree, exactly. Ridiculous.

You have a body that worked fine for years, decades. And then one day you start noticing it is not working the way it used to. You go to the doctor, and the doctor says you have an extra part, and you need surgery to remove the extra part. And, not to worry, the part isn't necessary. It was put in by the "manufacturer" and is really just an extra part. You go to specialist, because you want a second opinion, and the specialist says the same thing. You have an extra part, and you need surgery to remove the extra part. So you agree, and you let the doctor take out the extra part. And after when the doctor is done with the surgery and has taken out the part, there are all these other problems that now show up, that the doctors probably didn't tell you about, or didn't fully explain.

People who had their tonsils taken out because those were just extra pieces now have a greater risk of getting upper respiratory disease, a more severe problem than sore throats. People who had their appendix taken out have a greater chance of getting colon cancer. Just because we didn't know how important these parts were when doctors routinely took them out doesn't mean they are not important.

Many doctors see the body as a machine, like your car. Now, to you and me, it is obvious that the body is a lot more than just a machine like your car. This is important, because if your car breaks down, it is not going to fix itself, it is not going to get better without someone fixing it. This is how most doctors see the body. If it is broken, the only way to fix the body is to do something, because the body cannot heal itself. This is part of the Newtonian physics that was proven wrong in the 1920s, and medicine still uses it as if it were true.

Imagine for a moment that every night while you slept a mechanic came into your garage, and replaced any part of your car that was wearing down and not working correctly. Every time the fabric of the seats got a little worn, the mechanic would replace the seats. When the gauges got dirty, they would be replaced. When the engine started to wear and lose some power, the mechanic would replace the engine. Any time the tires became worn, the mechanic would change the tires. The brakes become worn, and the mechanic would replace the brakes. He did all this in your garage while you slept. This mechanic knew every hose, every wire, every computerized part, everything about your car.

Do you think you would ever have to worry about your car breaking down? No, of course not, because when it first started to break down, the mechanic would replace it.

This is kind of how you can think of the human body. And the mechanic is the inner wisdom, the inner wisdom that knows EVERYTHING there is to know about you, your body, and your mind. Everything. And every night, your inner wisdom goes to work on healing you and making you better. This inner wisdom is what quantum physics shows us as the sum of the parts equal to more than the whole.

All you have to do is make sure the mechanic has everything he needs. He will tell you what he needs, and you just have to make sure to do it. This is like your inner knowing. It tells you what it needs to make you well all the time. But if you don't listen, if you don't give your body the parts it needs to replace the broken-down parts, your inner wisdom cannot fix you. If the mechanic doesn't have an extra set of brake pads, he cannot replace the old worn-out ones.

Scientists understand that just because they don't know how to do something, that doesn't mean it is impossible. They know that current ways of thinking are always changing, always being improved upon. They know that their lack of knowledge does not make something so. The medical profession seems to think that if they don't know how to help you, it is impossible, that if they don't know how to do it, it cannot be done. They do not stay open to the constant changes and improvements being made in health care. They hold on to their old ways, and refuse to change until the evidence against what they practice is so overwhelming that they have no choice.

Medical symptoms and disease care is the least scientific group around. They base their theory on physics principles which were proven wrong 70 years ago. The medical symptoms and disease care system thinks everyone else should measure what they do with the medical symptoms and disease care measures, no matter how inappropriate it is. The medical symptoms and disease care system doesn't have to do double-blind studies on surgery and other things. But everyone else has to do double-blind studies on everything they do. The medical symptoms and disease care system holds on, fighting for their theories tooth and nail, until the evidence becomes so overwhelming, they are forced to change.

Medicine is not scientific at all.

Chapter 10

Leading Killer of Americans

The medical symptoms and disease care system actually admits to being the leading killer of people in America.

Now this is a pretty bold statement, one that many people would not want to make. And when you have the facts and references to back it up, it becomes more than a claim; it becomes the reality of what is so.

I will admit, right off, that this figure and statistic is not a "straightforward" admission, the way it appeared in Chapter 8. What I have done is to take all of the straightforward admissions, everything the medical profession has claimed, all the studies they have published, and simply added them up. Yep, that is it. The numbers and studies they published, they admitted to themselves, were simply added up. And when you add up the different numbers, it puts the medical symptoms and disease care system as the number one killer in the US.

If you take all the different numbers of people the medical profession has admitted to killing and add them up, the American medical system is the LEADING cause of death in the US. The medical system has indicated with their own numbers, their own studies, and their own publications, that they are killing more people in the US than anything, including cancer, heart disease, or any other disease.

Some people will try to use the argument that you can prove anything with statistics and studies. I couldn't agree more. And the statistics and studies I am referencing are the medical symptoms and disease care system's studies and statistics. They are the studies they did themselves. They are the statistics that they came up with themselves. The only thing they didn't do was add them up. And you can check the math yourself. The numbers add up.

I want to remind you: If the tobacco companies did a study that proved smoking was bad for you, you would have to believe it. Because their goal would be to prove that smoking is safe. If they funded a study that proved the exact opposite of what they wanted, something that did not make them look good, you would have to know it was for real.

The studies and statistics were gathered and admitted to by the medical symptom and disease care establishment. When they do a study that makes them look bad, you pretty much have to believe it.

So, yes, you can prove anything with studies and statistics. And it is easy to see that the AMA does not want the results published. Even with any doctoring and fudging that might have been done, these are the best results they could come up with, the best in terms of what doesn't make them look so bad.

The medical symptoms and disease care system admitted to killing people in different ways. They have tried to sweep the ugly truth under the rug by not admitting to the total number of people they kill in one place. Someone had to finally added up all their admissions and come up with some scary numbers.

Using the most conservative numbers, the number of people the medical symptoms and disease care system kills each year is 783,936 people. This makes the medical symptoms and disease care system the leading killer of Americans. That is over 2,000 people every day that the medical symptoms and disease care system kills. Every day, 2,000 people dead.

Imagine the headlines. "Six jumbo jets crashed today and everyone on board was killed." It would be everywhere. Then the next day, the same thing. Six jumbo jets fall from the sky and everyone on board is killed. You have a flight the next day. Would you fly? Every day, six jumbo jets fall from the sky and everyone on board is killed. This happens every day for a year. Every year for over five years. There would be no more jets to fly within a year or two, not to mention that, with a week of six jumbo jets crashing every day and everyone on board being killed, how long before you quit flying?

Here are the numbers and references:

Condition	Deaths	Cost	Author
Adverse Drug Reactions	106,000	$12 billion	Lazarou(1), Suh (12)
Medical Error	98,000	$2 Billion	IOM(4)
Bedsores	115,000	$55 Billion	Xakellis(5), Barczak (6)
Infection	88,000	$5 Billion	Weinstein(7), MMWR (8)
Malnutrition	108,000	-	Nurses Coalition(9)
Outpatients	199,000	$77 billion	Starfield(10), Weingart(14)
Unnecessary Procedures	37,136	$122 billion	HCUP(15,11)
Surgery-Related	32,000	$9 billion	AHRQ(13)
Total	**783,936**	**$282 billion**	

In 1999, Americans made more visits to natural health care providers than to medical doctors, and the number of visits has been going up ever since. If you searched the literature and really dug, you might be lucky if you found 10 people being killed by natural health care providers. So let's see, if you go to the Medical Symptoms and Disease Care system to try to get well, they kill 780,000 people every year. If you go to the natural health care providers, they kill maybe 10 people per year. What do you want to do first?

The natural health care field has conducted more studies than many of the medical symptoms and disease care system proving how well it works; they just aren't the faulty $100 million double-blind studies. They kill far fewer people per year. It is time to make natural health care the standard by which true health care is judged. It is time to wake up.

Over 780,000 people's lives are lost every year. This is more people killed than in any year of all of the wars the US has been in throughout all of history.

Now, if you take the higher numbers, you get almost one million people killed every year by the medical symptoms and disease care profession.

One million people killed every year. Get that for a minute. One million people dead. Every year. Killed needlessly because of the veil of protection the medical symptoms and disease care system has from the US government and the laws.

These statistics came from the Nutrition Institute of America and Gary Null, PhD, Carolyn Dean MD, ND, Martin Feldman, MD, Debora Rasio, MD, and Dorothy Smith, PhD, who gathered the data together from peer-reviewed medical journals.

As if this isn't bad enough, the Food and Drug Administration (FDA) feels the need to police and criticize natural health care providers and what they do, as part of protecting the American public from harm.

The FDA and others also spread rumors and lies that natural medicine is dangerous. What is more of a threat, one million people dead or ten? Yet the rumors persist. Have you heard the rumors that drinking too much water can kill you? The scares about some natural supplements that might have killed one person? WHOA! How about one million people EVERY YEAR!

The FDA *Consumer Reports* from September of 1998 lists the possible dangers of nutritional supplements.

The cover of the May, 2004 *Consumer Reports* magazine blares in bold type: "Dangerous Supplements!" Hello? What about the medical symptoms and disease care profession?

CBS news reported about dangerous sport supplements, and all the alleged reports of dangerous interactions between herbs and prescription drugs.

The list goes on and on. Why do you never hear about all the documented people killed by prescription drugs and the medical symptoms and disease care system? Instead, you hear that vitamins, herbs and water are bad, when you would be hard pressed to find ten people a year who have been killed by them, maybe even ten people ever.

Now, I will step out on a limb and say that the medical symptoms and disease care system kills over two million people every year. The number two killer in America is heart disease. This is an almost 100% preventable disease. One of the major contributing factors to heart disease is sugar and refined grains. Yet the medical symptoms and disease care professionals and the AMA still recommend that people eat these very two things to try to prevent heart disease. They recommend eating carbohydrates and cutting down on fats and protein, when fats and proteins are exactly what you need to prevent heart disease, specifically Omega-3 fatty acids in a one-to-one relationship with Omega-6 fatty acids. If it wasn't for the AMA's misinformation, heart disease would not kill 700,000 Americans per year.

Cancer is the third leading cause of death in the US, with over 500,000 people dying every year from cancer, and most cancer is 100% curable. I say the medical symptoms and disease care system is responsible for these deaths as well. Here is why:

The reason why you do not have all these proven natural therapies everywhere helping people heal themselves and get rid of the cancer is because of the medical symptoms and disease care system and their magic veil of protection. If they treat someone with chemo, surgery and radiation and the person dies, they say it was just the cancer. If you treat someone with anything else instead of the current "reasonable and customary" methods and the person dies, you will get sued and probably lose, even though the survival rate for getting medical symptoms and disease care treatment for cancer in the US is only about 50% overall.

Insanity is doing the same thing over and over again, and expecting a different result. If you do the same thing, you can expect the same result.

For over 30 years, Medicine has been trying the same thing, surgery, chemo and radiation to cure cancer. And 30 years later, they still have no cure. They have better surgery procedures, they have different chemotherapy agents, they have different machines for radiation, but they are still doing the same thing. It is like a fly hitting its head on the window, as it is trying to fly out the window. It comes at it from different angles. It comes at the window faster and slower. It takes a break. The fly may even try another window. But yet, it still doesn't get out. Why? It is doing the same thing over and over again. Yes, it is slightly different, but overall, it is the same thing.

Back then, medical symptom and disease care also thought the body was a machine. Like a clock, with no internal wisdom, nothing guiding it other than the Genes. So if the human body or "machine" screwed up, they had to fix it. If you "got" cancer, the medical symptom and disease care had to fix you. Like when your car breaks down. Your car does not fix itself, you must have someone fix it. So the tumor was this "thing" and it would make sense, that if you just cut out the tumor, things might get better, because the tumor was gone. And from their knowledge and perspective at the time, that made total sense.

One thing that needs to be remembered is that at one time chemotherapy, radiation, and surgery were not reasonable and customary either. They were new and unproven. Now, here is the interesting part. Chemotherapy, radiation, and surgery initially started being used based solely on an idea, a theory. You see, the medical symptom and disease care system had no other form of treatment for cancer, so these techniques were the only thing that was available, and they made some sense based on what knowledge they had at that time. No one double-blind study. They didn't do double-blind studies to compare chemo/radiation/surgery to other things, to prove it to be the most effective. Doctors started using these methods with only some case studies and a theory. And, by the way, the theory was based on Newtonian physics, which at that time had "only" been proven wrong 40 years ago.

Research shows that cancer cells grew quicker, and divided quicker, than normal cells. The medical community thought, Well, radiation kills cells that are dividing. The same thing with chemotherapy. It is a drug that kills ALL cells that are dividing. So since cancer cells divide quicker, they thought that radiation and chemotherapy might help kill more cancer cells then regular cells. And, in theory, it sounds great. Kill all the cells that are dividing. Cancer cells divide quicker, so they will likely die quicker. Yes, your body will have casualties of war. Other cells that are dividing will also die. But it will be best for the whole (so the theory went).

Doctors did that for a while, because they knew of nothing better to fight cancer with, and then it became reasonable and customary. Interestingly, no studies were done, no research. Doctors just did it because they had no other options. Nowadays, the studies they do have are case studies, or double-blind studies comparing one form of chemo to another or one form of radiation to another. They still have no double-blind studies proving chemo is better than any of the other ways of helping cancer heal. No double-blind studies that they think everyone else should do.

It is 40 years later, 30 years since the official "war on cancer" was declared, and we are still losing miserably. No known cures, nothing. The only thing the medical profession is saying is that we are getting better at curing people. They say this because statistics indicate that the survival rate is going up. Now, that is interesting. The survival rate is going up. What does that actually mean?

The only thing the AMA can state is that the survival rate is going up. You would think that this means more people are cured of cancer completely, and living a healthy normal life again, right? Wrong. The survival rate is the number of people who are alive five years after the time of diagnosis. Does this mean that people are living longer? That more people are cured than before? Or does this just mean that the diagnosis and detection of cancer is getting better?

Let me explain. Let's say a person starts developing a tumor. In one year, untreated, it is 1 cm in size. In two years, 2 cm in size, and after two years the person finally gets symptoms, obvious to anyone, that there is something wrong. So that person goes to the doctor, the doctor does some tests, and finds out that there is cancer. The patient goes through treatment and, four years, 364 days after the original diagnosis, the person is dead. The patient is not a cancer survivor. If that person had lived only one more day and then died, they would have been a cancer survivor. That is not even my point, but it is an interesting one. This person is dead six years and 364 days after the tumor started.

Now let's say that same person went to the doctor for a routine check-up a year earlier. This check-up included screening for the type of cancer they had. The doctor found the cancer early, and the person begin treatment. Five years and one day later, the person is still living. They are now a cancer survivor. This person who, if they had waited one year longer to visit the doctor, would now probably not be a cancer survivor. It is now only six years from when the tumor started. In the above scenario, the person lived six years and 364 days. But even if they die 364 days later from the cancer, they are still a cancer survivor. In both scenarios the person was alive for six years and 364 days. In one the person is a survivor, in the other they are not. The only difference is that the diagnosis was made earlier in the "survivor's" case, even though the cancer still killed them.

Everyone knows, and the medical profession seems so eager to tell us, that early detection is the key for treatment. Why? Because the survival rates are better if the cancer is detected early. The medical profession says this over and over again. They are getting great at early detection.

What I am saying is, I think the treatment does nothing to help people live longer. That, statistically, the reason survival rates are going up is because the medical profession is getting better at detecting cancer earlier. Since they detect the cancer earlier, the person has longer before the natural progression, if left unchanged, leads them to death. And that earlier detection time gets people pushed over the five-year mark to make them cancer survivors, even if they die from the cancer one day after the five-year mark from the date of diagnosis.

Cancer is looked at as this elusive thing, when in all actuality, it is something that happens every day in every person. You develop one million cancer cells in your body every day. And, every day, your body kills one million cancer cells.

What is cancer? Cancer is not a tumor. A tumor is the name given to a group of cancer cells. Cancer cells are mutated cells. And every day you develop about one million mutated cells in your body. And every day of your life, your body gets rid of those cancer cells. Even if you have a tumor, up until you got that tumor, every day of your life, your body developed one million cancer cells, and every day, your body got rid of them.

Your body is so amazing. Every second you produce 50 million new cells. Every second your body makes 50 million new cells. Every second your body rips apart the genetic code in 50 million cells. Every second it duplicates 50 million cells. Every second. Now, in that process, with SOOO many cells being made in one day, there is bound to be an error here and there. Imagine copying 50 million pieces of paper every second. Do you think you might make an error or two, or a million? Exactly. As your body creates 50 million new cells each second, there are some errors. And these errors are cancer cells. Your body created a system to deal with this, because it knows errors happen. So your immune system works every day to kill off these cancer cells.

What happens when you get a tumor is that your body does not kill off these cells that have divided wrong. Your body, for whatever reason, lets them grow. Most cells that are mutated grow and divide quicker than normal cells, so the damaged cells begin to grow and divide. And then you develop a tumor big enough to create medical symptoms and for the disease care system to detect and diagnose.

Now, wouldn't it make more sense to fix the reason why your body quit killing the mutated cells? What happened? Why did your body quit doing something it had done a million times each day for your entire life?

Better yet, if you got your body to start killing those mutated cells, those cancer cells, it wouldn't matter why it quit. Maybe why might make a difference to keep it from happening in the future, but it wouldn't matter now. Your body would be killing the cancer cells, and without any surgery, radiation, or chemotherapy, your body would heal itself, just as your body has done a million times a day in the past. But the question of why your body stopped killing these mutated cells is not addressed by the medical symptoms and disease care system.

In fact, your body's killing cancer cells is what the medical symptoms and disease care system ends up relying upon in the end. The medical system just looks at getting the cancer out, and who cares about why you stopped killing these cells yourself? They do their chemo, radiation and/or surgery and then, at the very end, they rely upon your inner wisdom. They hope that your body is able to get rid of any cancer cells that might be left.

The following idea is my theory, which is really no different than what the medical profession has, because they only have a theory as well. They only difference is that more people subscribe to their theory. Popular opinion is no measure of validity, because at one point in America it was popular opinion that burning people at the stake was a good idea.

Cancer does not metastasize and spread. Cancer does not pick up its bags, and travel somewhere and find a new home. You hear the doctors say, "We have to get it early before it metastasizes." Here is my theory:

This pulls back from the previous chapter about how your DNA does not cause you illness. There is part of your DNA that is constructively, with intent, mutating itself to try to better deal with the perceived environment. Every cell has the DNA needed to make any cell that is within your body and, at any one time, 50 million cells are mutating. So when cells mutate specifically with intent, they do so in more than one place. If one of these mutations that happened in multiple places doesn't end up serving the body, the body usually gets rid of these cells.

But if, for some reason, the body does not recognize the cancer cell as cancer, it will not get rid of the cells, and the body will not get rid of those mutated cells anywhere they are in the body. If these cells are left to grow, the body has a different blood supply, oxygen supply, and all sorts of other factors that are different in all the different parts of the body, so of course the cells will grow at different rates, and the tumor, or group of cancer cells, will show up in some places before others. If this continues, eventually you will see tumors in other parts of the body. They all started at the same time. No one moved or metastasized. That is why tumors can often seem to be of the same origin.

I am not saying no cancer metastasizes. I think some do. The body's lymph system is like a sewer system; its job is to filter out all the garbage, including cancer cells, from the lymph. Then your immune system has a concentrated place from which to launch its attack. This is very efficient. But sometimes the cancer cells can grow in these lymph nodes, wherever they are in the body.

This to me is also the reason why in so many people the cancer comes back later. The doctors never really dealt with why the body was not killing the cancer cells in the first place. They just focused on getting rid of the cancer.

If you have a plumbing leak and the bathroom floor is flooding with water, do you just keep mopping up the water, or do you find out why the water is on the floor and fix that? If the body is not getting rid of cancer cells, you are developing cancer cells in your body. Do you just keep killing the cancer cells, or do you look at why your body quit killing those cancer cells? After 30 years, the medical system still does not look for the reason why.

Most of the natural ways of treating cancer have an 80-90% cure rate, and this is usually with people the medical symptoms and disease care system has given up on. I think the numbers would be even better if natural practitioners got the "easy" cases as well.

This is why I say the medical symptoms and disease care system is responsible for most of the 500,000 deaths each year from cancer. They are withholding appropriate health care that has been proven more effective. They are using methods that are 30 years old, which have pretty much never been tested, and especially have never been tested in the way the medical community expects others to test their form of cancer treatment.

You might be asking yourself, why haven't you heard about two million Americans being killed every year? Why isn't it all over the papers and front page of the newspaper? I mean, natural health care gets better results, and yet you hear nothing. This is because most of these systems and the people who use them have been driven out of the country. Literally. Many people have practices set up in Mexico and the Caribbean, because they cannot practice in the US, even though their documented cancer cure rate is considerably higher than that of the medical symptoms and disease care system.

As I said, if you treat cancer with natural methods, and you have 99.9% of the people you see healed, you can still be sued and lose because of that one person who dies. And since you did not use traditional methods, you are liable. But if the medical symptoms and disease care system has 50% of their patients dying from cancer, and they use chemo, radiation and surgery, then no one is liable. The doctor has this magical veil of protection.

When this veil of protection started, the idea was good: Hold others to a standard set by the medical profession as, at the time, the medical profession was probably better than the natural methods being used. This faulty assumption was based on the fact that other systems were not nearly as popular and did not have the mega-bucks to do studies like the drug companies anyway. So it was decreed that the medical symptoms and disease care system was the standard to which "health care" was to be held and against which it was to be judged.

This meant that if you did anything that was not reasonable and customary, you could get into big trouble. If you did not do what most of the medical profession did, you could get into big trouble. And without even knowing it, the medical profession locked themselves into doing the same thing forever. Or maybe they did know. Either way, they destined themselves to doing the same thing forever.

What is reasonable and customary is what is being done. And you cannot do anything other than what is reasonable and customary. So if you discover something new, it is not reasonable and customary. You cannot do something that is new and cutting edge, because it is not reasonable and customary, unless you have a billion dollars to do a government approved study to prove the new way is better than the old.

I don't know about you, but I don't have a billion dollars in my spare change piggy bank that I can spend to prove that a natural form of cancer treatment works. Most other natural health care systems and groups do not, either, and the government is not going to give it to you. Out of $12 billion allocated every year by Congress to the National Institutes of Health, a mere $5.4 million goes to the Office of Alternative Medicine. There is not enough money allocated to do even one study on some natural method of healing. So unless you already make billions of dollars by selling your drugs, surgery, and procedures which kill 780,000 Americans every year, you cannot get your new method approved. No matter how great your natural method of healing may be, you cannot play by the rules that have been created.

The very system that was created to protect people is now actually killing them, at a rate of 780,000 Americans per year dead. It is time. The medical symptoms and disease care system needs to have its veil of protection lifted.

This can easily be done. Remove the reasonable and customary laws and let people choose for themselves. Let the statistics that have been proven by case study, which happens to be one of the most effective measurement tools for natural health care, be proof enough. It just isn't the double-blind $100 million study.

I personally would like to see natural health care become the reasonable and customary. There are more studies, and natural practitioners kill FAR FEWER people, about two million people fewer, and people are now making more visits to natural health care providers than to the medical profession. But I think that might be a step too big for America to take all at once, even though it makes the most sense.

A system that kills 780,000 people every year is no longer helping more people than it is hurting. People deserve the freedom to choose what they want. We are the country that espouses personal freedom as one of our greatest attributes. Give people back the freedom to choose for themselves.

Because the medical symptom and disease care system has such a veil of protection, it actually ends up postponing natural care that could actually help people. Many doctors know nothing of natural health care, and have no idea when it is appropriate to send some of their patients for natural health care. I say they are killing most of the people who die of some sickness or disease. With natural means, there are very few illnesses that cannot be helped. I have seen this personally, over and over again.

I say that the medical symptoms and disease care system kills over two million Americans per year. Two million lives gone, each year. The 750,000 unnecessary heart disease-related deaths from the inaccurate recommendations of the medical symptoms and disease care system, and the 500,000 people who needlessly die from cancer that is curable with natural methods, plus the 780,000 people the system directly kills, adds up to over two million people. The medical symptoms and disease care system is responsible for over two million deaths every year.

It is time to remove the protective veil from a group of people responsible for over two million American deaths every year. It is time to hold them accountable for their actions just like everyone else. It is time to give you the freedom of choice over your health care needs and wants. We now live in the Information Age, and people can easily get enough information to make educated choices themselves. The government does not have to protect people the way they once did.

Chapter 11

Eliminating Fear

To eliminate fear, you must understand where it comes from. This chapter will be about showing you where all the different forms of fear creep into your life, often without your even knowing it. In knowing where the fear comes from, you can avoid it.

The medical symptoms and disease care system preys on your fear of death. Fear of death is the second biggest human fear, second only to public speaking. And the medical symptoms and disease care system uses this fear to control you. If you don't get vaccinated, you will die. If you don't do this or that, you will die. If you don't get chemo and radiation when you have cancer, you will die. And on and on. They use this fear to get you to do what they think is best for you. The problem comes, as you now know, in that these things are not best for you.

As I made reference to earlier, when fear is the perception, you and your cells go into protection mode. This means you are not healing or growing. You cannot be. You are either in protection mode or growth mode. It is one or the other, and your perception of the outside environment determines which mode you are in. When the medical symptoms and disease care system uses fear to control people, they are almost guaranteeing that you will not heal.

That is why, in my opinion, the use of fear to control people is the single biggest damaging thing this system does. In my opinion, a huge portion of the two million people they kill every year die because of the fear they use. People are constantly in fear, and even on the really rare occasion that the surgery or drugs were helpful, the fear and protection state keeps the body from healing.

This is also true when fear is used to control people, or simply when fear is present. In America, we live in a culture of fear. In the media, the government, the nightly news, even our entertainment, fear is all pervasive. It controls and dominates our culture. When you perceive fear, you are in protection, survival, and struggle mode. When the environment is friendly, you thrive, grow, and heal.

Consider the constant supposed threat of terrorists, the latest form of fear that keeps people in the protection and survival state. We are constantly told that terrorists could be anyone, they could come from anywhere. What is the security threat level at this week? The three-year anniversary of 9/11 has just passed, and nothing has happened. No terrorists, no attacks, nothing.

Whether or not you like Michael Moore for his political views, he makes an undeniable, excellent case about how pervasive fear is everywhere—in the media, nightly news, government, everywhere.

Remember Y2K? All the hysteria, chaos and fear. The world will collapse! Midnight rolled around and nothing happened.

Or how about the myth about a razor blade in an apple at Halloween? There never was a razor in an apple. Never was there a razor. In the past 40 years, only two kids have ever been killed by Halloween candy, and they were poisoned on purpose by relatives.

Remember the smallpox, and biological threats of terrorists, and that everyone must get vaccinated and be careful opening your mail? Well, nothing ever happened.

Or how about AIDS? Remember all the fear and mass hysteria in the 80s? Deadly disease will spread and millions could soon be killed. The same number of people die from AIDS in the US each year as did in the 80s.

How about murder? We must fear being killed when, in fact, over the past couple years, the murder actually went down 20%, but the coverage of murder went up by 1500%.

And now They don't even need to give you a reason. The Justice Department often offers blanket alerts based on general threats. They are telling us to be afraid, and not even giving us a reason why.

The movie *Bowling for Columbine* shows anyone who is willing to move past the title and politics how fear is all-pervasive, and how fear is at the root of most of the problems everyone is trying to solve. Where does this fear come from? We ask for it, and the media and the government willingly give it to us.

There is nothing to fear. When people are in fear, they can be easily controlled. Fear is also what people "vote for" by what they watch on TV and what they give their attention to. It is simple to stop the fear. Remove yourself from the demand for this media, this fear. When you stop watching and being a part of this, the fear goes away. Yes, the media willingly feeds us the fear, but you do not have to consume it. And when you consume something other than fear, you and your cells grow and heal.

When the fear goes away, you can actually grow, prosper, and heal.

Your fear of death comes from the unknown. What will happen to you after you die? Are you eternal? Or do you just die? People do not want to just die, and not knowing what will happen causes the fear of death. I will show you what has to happen.

In Chapter 6 I talked about the intelligent force that drives genetic mutations with intent and purpose. This intelligence is the same intelligence that governs every process in your body. It is this inner wisdom that gives you life. It has been breathing life into you since before you were conceived.

Science knows that energy is neither created nor destroyed. The energy just transforms from one form of energy into another. Energy doesn't cease to exist; it goes on forever. The inner wisdom that gives you life is energy. It cannot cease to exist, either. It must go on forever. This inner wisdom is what many religions refer to as your spirit, the life force that gives you life. This inner wisdom is energy that continues after your body is gone. Said another way, your spirit, or the essence of you, continues after your body is dead. This inner wisdom was there before you were actually conceived, and will continue after your body is dead.

If you take the power of the inner wisdom, multiply it by infinity, take it to the depths of forever, you will barely have a glimpse of how powerful and far-reaching this force is. Death is nothing to fear, because your essence will continue.

I want to share with you now how the medical symptoms and disease care system knows nothing. And, for that matter, why the idea of treating and diagnosing is fundamentally flawed. Knowing how the medical symptoms and disease care doctors know nothing will help you break their bonds of fear. When they tell you that you only have X months to live, or there is nothing that you can do, you will know the truth. They do not know it all.

Of everything there is to know about the human body and mind, how much do we as humans know?

Seriously, take a guess How much do we know, as humans, about how our body and mind function?

I read somewhere that the AMA states that we as humans know 10% of everything there is to know and that can be known about humans. I personally think this is a super generous figure. Of EVERYTHING there is to know about how the body and mind work, we know 10%. So, to make it easy, I will go with this number.

Of everything that we know as humans— all the textbooks on anatomy and physiology, all the specialists in the heart, nose, throat, ear, foot, bone, endocrine, GI, lung, and on and on, all the geneticists, cancer researchers, all the people, all the books, all the specialists, in all of the different fields, all around the world, all the knowledge in DNA and RNA, all the knowledge around quantum

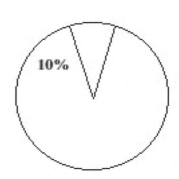

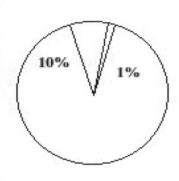

physics and the human body, all the knowledge of everything that is known, by all people, all around the world, everything there is to know about the human body, how much does any one human know about everything there is to know?

One percent. Again, you can see that that is a generous number. Of everything there is to know about, if one person could know one out of every 100 things, that would be pretty good.

Now, this 1% is of the 10% that we as humans collectively, actually know. Which means that is 0.1% of every thing there is to know. Any one person, at most, even with super-generous estimates, knows 0.1% of everything there is to know about the human body.

Let's say your car breaks down, and you bring your car to a mechanic. He opens the hood, looks at the engine, and says to you. "You know, all I really know is less than 0.1% about how this car works, but let me take a stab at it. Let me see if I can't figure out what is wrong and fix it." What will you to do? You will take your car elsewhere.

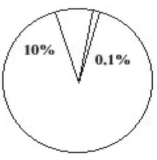

But that is exactly what we do with our bodies. We go to someone who knows less than 0.1% about how our body works, and want them to tell us what is wrong, and fix us. Or, we think with our own minds we can figure out what is wrong, and then with that knowledge of what is wrong, fix the problem ourselves.

This is the intellect or the conscious mind. It is impossible for the intellect to know what to do, to know anything about anything. OK, it's not that extreme but, for sure, when it comes to the human body, the intellect really knows less than 0.1% about how the body works. And trying to figure out which symptom is which with that intellect is like the mechanic, trying to figure out what is wrong with your car, and only knowing 0.1% about how it works. Almost impossible.

You have access to a much greater knowledge, and it comes from within. No one can give it to you or take it away; it is yours and always has been. This inner wisdom or inner knowing knows everything about you. It is the power that created you and gives you life, every moment of every day. This inner knowing knows 100% of what is going on and what you need to do, and you have direct access to this inner knowing.

This inner knowing is accessed through your heart center. Joseph Chilton Pearce in his book, *The Biology of Transcendence*, has an entire section describing the existence of the physiological heart brain, and how this heart brain is our connection to the inner knowing that runs our body and mind, the inner knowing that knows 100% of everything about you. By centering your focus on your heart center, you can actually listen to what your inner knowing is saying to you.

I will share more about this with you later, so don't worry if you didn't fully get it. I will have you get it later. The point of sharing about your heart brain now is to show you that you have direct access to that which knows 100% about you. You do not have to fear death or misdiagnosis or the medical profession and their threats—I mean, predictions. You have direct access to that which knows 100% about you, your health, and your life. The doctors know less than 0.1% about you, your life, and your body. This inner knowing knows 100% about what you need. You will have nothing to fear or worry about as you listen to this inner knowing.

Let's look for a minute at some of the things this inner wisdom does. There are:

- Six feet of DNA in every cell in your body
- 70 trillion cells in your body that are 1/1000 of an inch in size
- 100,000 chemical reactions happening in your body every second
- 50 million cells in the body being replaced every second
- 20 million red blood cells alone being replaced every second
- 40 billion bits of information being processed in the brain every second.

This is what your inner wisdom does, and more. The inner wisdom takes you from two half-cells at conception and creates a human with 70 trillion cells. This inner wisdom knows what it will take for you to be well, and it tells you. The problem is, you don't listen.

You are somewhere eating the best food, and you know you are full and should stop eating, but what do you do? You keep eating. You are up late at night watching a movie or working, and there are about 10 more minutes before you are finished. You are so tired, you know you should go to bed, but there are only 10 minutes left, so you stay up. You know that sugar is bad for you, and you shouldn't eat it, yet you do anyway. You inner wisdom is constantly telling you what it wants to be well. The problem is that you do not always give the inner wisdom what it wants.

The inner knowing will always tell you what it needs. It will tell you what it doesn't want. And the inner knowing will never lead you astray. It knows 100% about you and your life. There is nothing to fear when you are following your inner knowing.

The fear of death can also be dispelled by more clearly understanding what contributes to someone dying. I have noticed something very interesting. In the home of every person who was dying you can find the same thing. All the people who are dying are all putting this same thing into their body every day, sometimes 3-5 times a day. If there was something that you found in the home of every person who was dying, and they were putting it into their body up to five times a day, wouldn't you begin to wonder if that is what is killing them? I know I did. And that is exactly the conclusion I came to—that this thing all dying people are taking is in fact contributing to their death.

What is this one thing? It is drugs, both prescription and over-the-counter drugs. Every single person who is dying is taking multiple drugs up to five times a day. Interesting. Drugs do not add to your health; they only treat symptoms. Drugs are a contributing factor in causing death.

You are beginning to see how death is less and less mysterious, how it isn't even actually death, but more of a transformation, moving from one energy form to another.

If a doctor ever says "there is nothing that can be done," there is no need to fear, because this simply isn't true. What that doctor means is, "there is nothing I know that you can do." We just established that they know very little about anything, so just because there is nothing that they know to do probably means you are better off. You can find the things they don't know about.

Or if you are ever unlucky/lucky enough to hear from a doctor "you have X months to live," they don't know anything. They are totally guessing based on people who are different than you. Your beliefs are powerful. And if you fall for the trap of believing the doctor, your cells will respond to that belief. You and your cells will act as if you will die in X months, and probably will. So believe whatever you want to believe. But choose your beliefs wisely. They will greatly impact your future.

You are beginning to see how you can apply the knowledge of your inner knowing. Know that the medical symptoms and disease care system knows nothing. OK, 0.1%, which is essentially nothing. Trust your inner knowing over anyone in the outside world, including me. Be careful who and what you believe. If the belief doesn't empower you and help you get what you want, don't believe it. Believe the inner knowing of your body, and what it has to say.

I want to be clear; Do not stop going to the medical symptoms and disease care system because you are afraid they know nothing, or because you are fearful they will kill you. All those are very good and plausible reasons, but if that was the outcome, what I am offering would be no better than them. Quit going to the medical symptoms and disease care system because you now know better. You are informed and want what is best for you. You are listening to your inner knowing and it tells you to go elsewhere. Your inner wisdom tells you to do something else.

Chapter 12

The Biggest Lie . . .
We Tell Ourselves:
It Won't Happen To Me!

"It is not going to happen to me." You need to get real about this. As surely as your dropping an apple causes it to fall, if you do nothing about your health, you will lose it.

There are certain principles of the universe that happen, always, with certainty. If you drop a rock, it will fall. Gravity works all the time, with certainty, and without fail. Every time. No matter how much you don't want the rock to fall when you drop it, the rock will fall. No matter if you really believe the rock will not fall, it still will. It does not matter if you think the rock shouldn't fall, or the rock doesn't deserve to fall; the rock will fall if you drop it.

If you do nothing to take care of your health, you will not be healthy forever. This is as unbendable and immutable as dropping the rock. It will happen; your health will get worse, if you do not take care of it.

I am not saying you need to take care of your health. That is a choice that is up to you. What I am saying is, if you do not take care of your health, you will lose it. Even if you don't think you deserve to, and you don't think you should, and you don't want to believe you will. If you don't add to your health, you will lose it. It is as simple as that.

The medical profession does not have the answers, either. They are not going to give you health. They do not have anything that adds to your health. They do not have anything to help you heal. They are exclusively treating symptoms and disease, and when you get rid of symptoms and disease, you are not left with health.

If you do not keep adding to your health, you cannot rely on the medical symptoms and disease care system to help you get your health back. They are only good for managing symptoms and disease, often producing more negative effects than the thing they are trying to help you with. One of the negative affects is killing over 700,000 Americans every year. The system holds no long-term solutions to your health. The medical symptoms and disease care system has never offered permanent solutions to improving your health, only quick patches, fixes that don't last, and attempted control by prescribing drugs for the rest of your life. The medical symptoms and disease care system has not offered solutions to your health, and probably never will.

So don't wait until your health gets so bad that you are forced to do something about it. If you wait that long, it becomes harder to improve your health. Begin adding to your health, and you will not end up in any situation where you are forced to take care of your health. Good health will get you everything you want—peace, freedom, happiness, better relationships, more money, peace of mind, abundant energy, feeling great all the time. This list is really as long as you want to make it. The list in Chapter 3 is another place for you to review and see what is really possible. If you add to your health, you will have access to everything you want.

Section 1 review

- If you have symptoms, it does not mean you are sick
- If you don't have symptoms, it does not mean you are healthy
- There is no one thing that you have to do to be well
- Being old does not mean being helpless and decrepit. Not being healthy makes you old and decrepit
- There is a really high cost to pay if you are not doing what it takes to be well. The lon- and short-term hidden benefits, as you now know, are much better than the immediate benefits of not being healthy
- There is no one cause of symptoms or disease. There are many contributing factors, and everyone is different. If you choose to look, remember that you are looking for the major or key contributing factors
- Treating doesn't work, because it has been based on the flawed theory of one cause and one cure. There never will be cures, only what works for individual people
- Viruses, bacteria and parasites do not make you sick. You have to be unhealthy before the viruses, bacteria or parasites can make you sick
- Your DNA does not dictate your health. Your belief systems and perception of the world outside you hugely determines your health and life
- The medical symptoms and disease care system kills millions of Americans each year. Even using conservative statistics, millions die
- The medical symptoms and disease care system has a magic veil of protection, and it is now time for it to be removed. Any organization that kills millions of Americans every day no longer deserves a veil of protection
- The medical symptoms and disease care system is not scientific. They hold others to different standards than themselves; they refuse to change even when the evidence would say otherwise
- The medical symptoms and disease care system knows less than 10% about you and your body. Any one individual knows less than 0.1% about you and your body
- Your inner wisdom knows 100% about you and your body. It knows how to make you healthy. It is only a matter of listening to your inner knowing, which communicates through your heart brain.

SECTION TWO

The Key To Being Well and Healthy
Bazuji

Chapter 13

It Is All About Who You Are Being, Not What You Do or Have

Everyone and their grandma is telling you what to do. There is this book, and that book, and the second edition book telling you what to do. The biggest reason all these books and videos, and information are failing is that they are all focused on telling you what to do. They are not addressing the place to start, the place that will make the difference: who you are being.

You see, there is this phenomenon in life and here is how most of the people in the world think it operates.

They go out and do things to get things to have stuff. Then when they have enough stuff, they believe, that will make them be a certain way—happy, fulfilled, satisfied, etc. But when you do this, what happens? Many of you can directly relate to this. You have done what you were supposed to do, you have the stuff you want, and it does not fulfill you, make you happy, or any of the other things it promised to do. For the first month, it might have been great. Then there was this void again.

The three circles on the next page represent how life actually happens.

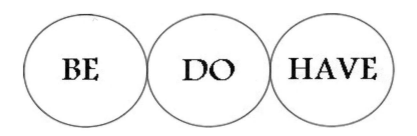

Who you are being leads to the things you do, and to what you eventually have. Life works by going from who you are being, which will lead to what you are doing, and then to what you have.

What you have does not make you fulfilled or happy. It may temporarily, but then you need something more, and more, and more and more. If who you are being, is not fulfilled or happy, or satisfied, or all of them, you will always have this void and need more.

Having health and being well is easy. Anyone can do it. In fact, almost everyone knows what to "do" to be healthy. But how many people actually do it? Not very many, because it is about who you are being, that makes the difference.

Let me give you an example: Lottery winners. Many people have heard about lottery winners—big millions of dollars winners. Within a few years, they are broke. If they had millions of dollars, how did they go broke within years? They didn't change who they were being. They were still thinking like a poor or middle-class person, and so they ended up doing what the poor and middle class do. Who you be leads to what you do. What these lottery winners did dictated what they had. They had what poor and middle-class people have. What you do dictates what you have.

One more example: Weight loss. You go out and do the things necessary to lose weight, and then you have weight loss. You now weigh less. Then, after a couple months, or a year or two, what happens? You are right back where you were. You focused on what to do, and you did it. You then had what you had, weight loss. But you never changed who you were being. You went back to your old way of being. And then who you were being dictated what you did and what you had. Your being brought you back to doing certain things. Then, doing those things led to what you have—weight gain.

This pattern is all too common. All of us have either done this or know many people who have. It is because most people focus on the doing. What you do will not lead to permanent results.

Who you are being leads to what you do, and to what you have. This is how the flow of life works. In fact, anywhere you are stuck in life, this little understanding can help to get you unstuck. Any area of your life you are stuck in or trying to change without success can often be helped with this. Most people focus on what to do: What I do, what do I do?" They then do something for a bit and have some results. They then go back to the way of being that they never changed, and end up with the same old results. You have to change your way of being in order to make permanent changes in any area of your life. And changing the way you think is the easiest way I know of to change who you are being.

The key is, who do you have to be? More importantly, how do you become that way? How do you change who you are being? That is exactly what you are doing with this book. It is helping to shape your thinking. You see, your thinking is one of the big things that comprises who you are being. Your thinking is what leads you to make your choices. Your thinking is the major thing that gives you who you are being.

The first section of this book was all about understanding reality, knowing what was made up, from what was real. In doing that, we created space to actually allow you to think differently.

Imagine you have a canvas that is full of paint and has a picture already on it. How hard is it to put something new on that canvas? If you started with a blank canvas, wouldn't it be easier to paint a picture? Absolutely. It would be so much easier to paint a picture on a blank canvas.

The same is true about how you think, and who you can be. You have lived a full life. You have filled up your "canvas of life" with many things. And if you want something different, it is easier to start with a blank canvas. That is what you just did. In getting rid of all the misunderstandings in the way you think, you have a blank canvas.

This section is about giving you new possible ways of thinking. With these new ways of thinking, who you are being will start to automatically change. But there is one little catch.

If you have been putting layer upon layer upon layer of paint on your canvas of life, you will end up with a thick layer of dark brown on your canvas. There will be no room to paint anything new. When you clean the canvas of your life, sometimes it is stained. Or it isn't totally blank, because you had so much stuff on it. Some people need a little more help. For many of you, this book is all you will need to change your way of thinking, to change who you are being. After reading this book you will be being and doing things that are healthy, and that will lead to your having health and well being.

Some of you might need a little extra help to clear the canvas. What I am about to share can help you make a big difference in your ability to follow through and make the changes you want to make, if your inner knowing wants a little boost.

This extra help comes in the form of shifting your thinking on four things: your driving forces or values, strategies and decision making, negative and stored emotions, and limiting decisions or faulty beliefs. Let me explain these.

Driving forces are what it is that is important to you. What is behind your making the choices you make? What you value, and these driving forces can easily be changed.

Strategies are the processes you go through to make choices, the ease and way you make decisions, and whether or not the decisions serve you and get you what you want.

Negative emotions and stored past emotions are experiences that are getting in the way of your life now. You had some emotion, and never let it go.

Limiting decisions are choices you make that reduce or limit the number of choices available to you in the future. They are faulty beliefs you formed that are shaping your health and life.

I have created four CD sets for those of you who want a little extra help with who you are being around health or anything else in your life, to easily help you change and eliminate these things directly. Your reading this book is doing a lot of this already, but if your canvas was really full to begin with, it might take a little more. You can also use these CDs to change areas of your life outside of health and well being, such as your career, relationships, family, or just about anything you want.

Driving forces are the things that are important to you, what you value, what you hold in high regard. Driving forces affect you because they are formed on a subconscious level. They then influence your choices and decisions, usually without your even knowing it. These driving forces are what is important to you, and they shift and change over time. The driving forces you have now you can easily change, IF you want to change them.

Having kids can change your values. Before you have kids, there are certain things that are important to you. Then, after you have kids, you have a whole other set of things that are important to you. You are the person who shifts your values, either by situational events or by choosing something new.

Your driving forces, in part, are just how you think, what you make a priority. You could say that your values are what shape the way you think.

If health and well being are not important to you, you will not make choices to support your health and well being. You will choose to do other things that are more important to you.

Knowing this, you can simply choose to make health more important. You can choose to make health and being well something that is more important to you. For some people it is this easy. For others, this CD set will make it that easy.

Strategies are processes you go through before you do anything. Whether or not you realize it, before you make a decision or do anything there is a process you go through every time. For some people, it is as simple as: See it, and buy it. Others have to think it over. Still others have to ask their family and friends what they think. This process is the same for similar choices. You probably have about 10 strategies that you use over and over. This includes how you make decisions. You can and do change your strategies through out your life, often unconsciously.

When you become aware of these strategies and ways you make decisions consciously, you can easily change them. You can use a different one, one that works better. For example, if your strategy for buying something is that you see it and like it, so you buy it, that might not work so well, unless you are rich. Even then it might not work so well. But if you knew this, you could then change this strategy. You could change this strategy to something that worked better for that situation, so that you don't buy things impulsively you don't need or want and then regret it later. This CD set helps you become aware of the strategies you have developed and how you make decisions, and then shows you how to easily change them to something that better serves you.

Negative emotions and past stored emotions are events that are impacting you in a negative way today. They are getting in the way of your having what you want. Stored emotions, especially if they are from really traumatic events in the past, can cause you huge health problems. There are so many different systems and techniques and theories about how to get rid of stored emotions, they can make your head spin. What I have on this set of CDs is the easiest and quickest way I know of to release stored past negative emotions.

Limiting decisions or faulty beliefs are decisions that you make that cut off the number of choices that are available to you now and in the future. For instance, you might believe that viruses make you sick. In that case, whenever you know you were exposed to a virus, you get sick. Or it might be something more impactful, such as deciding/believing that you can't do something. What occurs for the rest of your life is that you are not able to do it. Or you decide/believe "I'm not smart enough," or "I am not athletic," or "I am not good enough." Then you spend the rest of your life "proving" this. You can have more than one of these limiting decisions or faulty belief systems and, in fact, often there are more than one.

Limiting decisions are often the major reason why people sabotage themselves. People know what to do, but the second they are not paying attention they are unconsciously doing something they know is not good for them. Behaviors like this are often just limiting decisions at work.

When you remove the limiting decisions, the self-sabotaging behavior often stops.

You can have limiting decisions or faulty beliefs in a good/bad way as well. You might say "I can't do it," and then spend the rest of your life overachieving, driven at all cost to prove you can do it. But no matter how much you do, you never quite feel as if you have proven yourself enough. You always have to do more.

When you look, you can find these patterns everywhere, and there are only a couple of places out there that deal with these. The easiest, most effective way that I have found to get rid of these limiting decisions and faulty belief systems is by listening to this CD set.

These four sets of CDs help you produce permanent lasting results in your life. People from as young as age 4-7 to as young as age 143 can use them. It literally is so simple that a child can do it. These CDs are for those who want or need that little extra help, and for those who want to use them for other areas of their life. These CD sets can be purchased at my website, www.bazuji.com.

Another thing you can do to help clear the canvas is to call on the "I AM" force or the creative powers of the universe to help. Ask God, your higher Self, visualize these powers, or whatever works for you. To me, visualizing is asking the Higher Intelligence that knows all, without using words. In fact, asking for what you want often helps with anything, whether it is asking other people or your Creator. Just ask, and it is a lot more likely that you will get what you want.

Now, there is a secret to this asking/visualizing. The key is feelings. Feelings have so much power. If you just ask for the sake of saying the words, or visualize just for the sake of seeing the picture, it is less likely that you will see results from this. Now, if you put feeling, love and life into the request/picture, the results you get will go through the roof.

My favorite book of all times is about how to put the creative powers of the universe to work for you, whether it is for healing, business, relationships, or anything else you want, especially enlightenment and transcendence. It is the third volume of *The "I AM" Discourses* by St. Germain, available from 1-847-882-1911. I even like this little book more than my CDs. Reading this book is more work than listening to my CDs, but worth it.

This book actually gives you the how-to, the fundamentals of what you actually do to produce miraculous results in your life, unlike a lot of other books that just tell you stories and hint around the subject.

Creating Desire – A Natural Expression for Health and Life

Creating a natural desire for anything is easy. You can choose to shift your thinking. You can get more information to help. You can just make a decision. Decide and know that there is no going back on your decision. Or you can do all three.

When you have a natural burning intense desire for something, you are much more likely to follow through with it. That is one of the big benefits of desire. When you use it for yourself, instead of against yourself, it is great. I have been showing you how to shift your thinking; I have been giving you information. You can just decide, now: I am being healthy and well. Period. No going back. No turning around and deciding this is not for you.

You can also get the support of people around you, by telling them, and asking them to support you, even when you tell them not to.

For example, tell your spouse that you want to work out on Tuesday and Thursdays. Then, give them permission to tell you there are no excuses, so that in the future, when you say "I don't want to go," they can call you on it. Your spouse can say "Remember when you told me..." You cannot change your mind because you told your spouse "even if I change my mind, don't let me." Then your spouse or friend or whomever can do what it takes to get you to go.

CHAPTER FOURTEEN - WHAT HEALTH IS

Creating *desire* as a key to getting what you want.

The book *Think and Grow Rich* by Napoleon Hill talks about this as well. You can use this book for anything in your life. It is just that getting-rich books sell more copies.

In summary, the key is who you are being. You can do stuff all day. You can have all the stuff in the world. But if you don't start with who you are being, you will end up back in your old ways. Your way of being gives you what you do and what you have. The biggest things that affects who you are being, is the way you think.

Be conscious of the thoughts you have all day long. Get rid of the ones you don't want. Change how you think about what is possible. Being someone who thinks in a whole new way, creates the you that you want to be.

Chapter 14

What Health Is

What is health? I actually want you to stop for a moment and think about what health is to you. If you were healthy, what would it look like? What would it be like?

So what did you come up with?

Kind of tough, wasn't it? Never really gave it much thought before. Most people haven't.

I want to take you on a sidetrack for a second that will come back around. Imagine you have a bow and arrow. It is real, tangible, right now in your hands. You can feel it and see it. There it is. Now, there is a target. I know what it is, it is a specific target, and I am NOT going to tell you what it is. OK, go ahead, shoot your bow and arrow and hit the target. Go ahead, shoot.

Did you hit the target? You have no idea if you hit the target or not. You don't know what the target is. What are the odds of your hitting the target when you don't know what it is? Slim to none. If you don't know what the target is, if the target can be anything, it makes it really hard to hit the target.

Well, what is health? What does health look like? And, most importantly, if you were actually healthy, what would that be like? What would be happening, what would be going on?

Interesting, isn't it? Most people in the world have no idea what the target of health looks like, yet everyone is trying to hit it. And even if they did hit it, they probably wouldn't know they hit it, because they don't know what the target of health looks like.

So create a target for yourself. Create a target that you want. I will give you some suggestions for the target in a later chapter. You can take them or leave them, use some and add any of your own you want. The beauty of this target is that you get to say what it is. And you can change your target later if you want.

For now, just begin thinking about what you want your target to be. When you are well, what is that going to be like for you?

Shining the light on the darkness

I will present a new way to look at what health is, to look at health for what it really is.

First a metaphor: light and darkness. What is light? What is darkness? With those questions, imagine you have a room where the lights are on, and there is a couch, a table, some chairs, and pictures on the walls. Now, if you were to turn off the lights, the room would be dark.

Where did that darkness come from? Was it hiding somewhere before it came into the room? Did it come from somewhere? You might be saying to yourself "those are silly questions. The darkness wasn't hiding anywhere. It didn't come from anywhere. The darkness doesn't exist. It is simply the absence of light."

Now, going back to that room, how do you get rid of the darkness? How do you get the darkness in that room to go away? Do you vacuum it out? Do you cut it out? Do you have some procedure or vitamin you can throw at the darkness to get the darkness to go away? Of course not! Everyone knows that to get rid of the darkness in the room, all you have to do is turn on the light. So when you turn on the light, where does the darkness go?

Does the darkness slip out under the door? Does the darkness hide under the rug? Does the darkness pile up in the corner? Does the darkness hide behind the pictures? Of course not. The darkness doesn't "go" anywhere, because the darkness doesn't exist. The darkness is not a thing. The darkness is not a physical thing with physical properties. It is simply the absence of light. That is it.

Take all the darkness in the world, and with one little candle, you will be able to see. You will have light. Darkness doesn't exist. It is not really a physical thing. It is what is left in the absence of light.

Now, most things in the universe operate on this principle of thing and no-thing. Energy is the thing. The absence of energy is no energy. Heat is the thing and cold is the absence of heat, sound is the thing and silence is the absence of sound, health is the thing and symptoms and disease are the absence of health.

Have you ever stood next to an outside air conditioner on a hot day when the air conditioner was running? If so, do you remember what you felt? You would feel heat; you would feel hot air coming out of the air conditioner, because the air conditioner does not make cold air, what the air conditioner does is to take the heat out of the air. It takes the heat out of the room, and forces it outside. That is why you need part of the air conditioner to be outside, and part of it to be inside, so it can take the heat out of the room, and then what is left is cool air.

Heat and cold. Heat is the physical thing, and cold is what is left when you take away heat.

Health and disease are the same. Health is the physical thing, and symptoms and disease are the absence of health.

Most people have a definition of health which is that health is just the absence of symptoms and disease. Many already know that health is more than just the absence of symptoms and disease. But what is health really, then?

From the beginning, the medical symptoms and disease care system got health and symptoms mixed up. They started treating symptoms and disease as the physical thing, and believed that health was what would be left when the disease was gone. Most forms of health care, including many "alternative and natural health care systems," are still trying to get rid of the symptoms and the disease, and hoping that you are left with health. They have been trying to cut the darkness out of the room, they have been trying to vacuum the darkness out, to do something to get the darkness to go away. They have been bringing vitamins and needles into the room to try to get rid of the darkness. They have been adjusting the furniture and moving it around to try to get rid of the darkness. And, as you know, it is futile to try to do anything to get the darkness out of a room without turning on the light. It is simply a matter of turning on the light, and the darkness will go away.

Now, in all actuality, health is a physical thing. Health is a tangible thing that must be dealt with. Health is the substance that, when increased, will allow the symptoms and disease to go away, the symptoms and disease to disappear. When you increase your health enough, your symptoms and disease will go away, just as when you turn on the light, the darkness goes away.

What happens when you turn on a light in a dark room? Yes, you all know, the darkness goes away. And if the light is not bright enough, if you don't have enough light, there are still shadows, right? When you turn on a light in the room, much of the darkness goes away. And if the light is not bright enough, there are still some shadows in the room.

To equate this to health, the shadows in the room are symptoms and disease. The medical symptoms and disease care system has created different labels and boxes for all the different types of shadows. They have measured, labeled, and quantified many different aspects of the shadows. They do this in the hope that if they can get enough information about the shadows, they can figure out how to treat them, how to get rid of the shadows.

As you know, treating a shadow without turning on the light is ridiculous. Trying to cut out the darkness, or treating it with some chemical, cream, pill, lotion or potion, is not going to do anything to get rid of the darkness. Absolutely nothing. The way to treat the shadow is not to treat the shadow. The way to get rid of the shadow is to turn on the light.

The way to heal your symptoms and disease is to turn on your health, to add to the level of health in your body, in your mind, in your being. When you add to your health, the symptoms and disease will cease to exist.

All the information that people acquire about the symptoms and disease is perfectly relevant, in the field of symptoms and disease management. There are many symptom and disease care specialists out there.

If you have a room full of shadows, you can measure the shadows, find out how long they are, how wide they are, measure the angles of the corners, the degrees of the curves, and how dark the shadows are. You can find out all kinds of information about each shadow, tons of information. What happens when you turn the lights on brightly enough in that room?

How relevant did all the information that you gathered about those shadows become? Did you have to know all the information about those shadows in order to increase the light in the room? Did you have to know anything about them whatsoever to increase the light in the room? Would the shadows still go away if you turn the light on brightly enough? Yes, absolutely, you are right. The shadows, without your needing absolutely any information about them, would go away when you turn on the light.

When you increase your health, when you add to your health, your symptoms and disease will go away. When you add enough to the amount of your health, symptoms and disease will go away. You do not have to know the label, the diagnosis, or the numbers about why you have symptoms and disease. You just have to turn on your health.

Some people have gotten a little smarter lately, and have gotten flashlights and started treating symptoms and disease by shining their flashlight on the shadow. When you shine a flashlight on a shadow, it goes away.

People have found great ways to increase the health in a certain area of the body through something that they do. This is great. And what I am pointing at with this book is: Turning on the floodlights. Better yet, bringing the sun into the room, because the sun, as you know, is bigger than the earth. If the sun were in the room, it would be everywhere, the light would be everywhere, and no darkness would exist. This is what I am pointing towards. This also happens to be the easiest and simplest way currently available to improve your health and well being.

Chapter 15

How To Get
Health and Well Being

Adding to your level of health is the *key*.

Here is an even better metaphor for health than the light and darkness metaphor: a bucket of water. You might be thinking: How can a bucket of water tell me anything about health? Great question, and here is the answer:

The bucket represents your body, your mind, your "being-ness," if you will. The water represents your level of health. What happens is that we all come into life with unique buckets. Written on the inside of your bucket is a list of all the symptoms and diseases that you are predisposed to—NOT destined to—but have a tendency to get. These are all written on the inside of your bucket. This is your DNA.

When you were born you had a certain level of water in your bucket. Most people were born with their bucket mostly full. That is why most babies and children seem to be healthier than adults. Any symptoms or diseases that are written on the inside of your bucket *above* your water level, are the symptoms and disease you express. You will experience all the symptoms and disease above the water level in your bucket.

The interesting part to me about all of this is that almost every one of us has symptoms that are above the water level of health. These are the same as the early warning symptoms I talked about earlier, like fatigue, bad eyesight, low energy, allergies, headaches, and other minor symptoms. They are your body asking you in a little louder voice to listen. Many of these symptoms that you express are symptoms that you ignore because you think they are just part of life. These symptoms I am talking about are things that you probably don't even know you have. Why do I say that? Because these symptoms are symptoms you don't even think are symptoms. They are symptoms that you think are just how it has to be. Let me give you an example.

When you wake up in the morning, do you spring out of bed, full of energy and vitality? Or do you hit the snooze bar two, three, or even nine times before you get out of bed? This, my friend, is a symptom. It is something that you think is part of life, part of working hard, part of whatever, and you accept it as the way it is, when it is nothing more than a lack of health. Because if you were healthy, you would wake up in the morning and get out of bed easily, with abundant energy.

Are you in a good mood all the time? Happy and fulfilled? Your moods are in direct relationship to your health, and when you are not as healthy as you could be, you are not as happy or happy as often as you could be, because of your lack of health. Happiness is just a certain chemical state in your body. Emotions are literally just different chemical reactions in the body. Different chemicals present in different amounts, and this is what produces different moods and emotions. That is why the medical profession gives drugs to try to change peoples' chemistry when they are depressed. If you can change the chemistry correctly, the moods and emotions of that person will change. If you are not abundantly happy and happy most of the time, that is a symptom.

As you go through the day, do you have high levels of energy to do whatever you want to do? Do you have energy levels to carry you right through the day? Or do you get sluggish and tired during parts of the day, especially after lunch? This is a symptom.

Do you experience stress? This is a symptom as well. Why is it that one air traffic controller goes home stressed out of his mind, and another air traffic controller sitting right next to him goes home perfectly fine? What is the difference? It is not the job. They both have the same job. The difference is how the individual people respond to the different situations. The healthier you are, the less stress you experience, no matter what is happening in the environment.

There are many more things, just like this, that many people accept as something they "have to" have, something they just must deal with because of circumstances. And this is simply not true.

The full potential of health, to me, is that of a four- year-old child.

When is the last time someone had to fight you to get you to go to bed at night? When is the last time someone had to bargain with you to get you to take a nap? When is the last time you ran to the car, just because you could? Or even better, had a contest to see who could run "over there" the quickest, and then when you got there, had a contest to run back to exactly where you started? Or just ran anywhere, simply because you could and because you were in love with life, and wanted to do as much as possible? You don't see kids getting up in the morning, rubbing their eyes, scratching their butts, staggering around with their cup of juice, trying to read their Fisher-Price books before they wake up. When kids get up, they are up, ready to take on the day. This is starting, and I mean only starting, to point to what having health really and fully means.

What you and most other people have done up until now, because we did not know anything better, is to take a symptom that is written above the water-line in the bucket and move it down below the water-line. And presto, magic, no more symptom. The symptom was treated and now it is gone. In the beginning, this works. What happened to the water level in the bucket when you treated the symptom and moved it lower in the bucket? That's right, nothing. Nothing happened to your level of health. Or, if anything, the treatment of the symptom decreased your health.

After a while the symptoms get all crowded and nudge around to make more room, and end up pushing some other symptom or disease above the water level on top because all the symptoms below need more space. This is why people who treat their symptoms are constantly having new symptoms they need to treat. Whether they treat their symptoms naturally, or with drugs and surgery, they are constantly taking more pills, more potions and lotions to treat their symptoms, and more keep coming. After they are done treating a particular symptom, they have done nothing to increase their health, and more symptoms are there, poking up above the water level of health.

What happens in life is that we put holes in our bucket. We do things that put "holes in the bucket," and then the water leaks out. As the water leaks out, more and more symptoms and diseases come up above the water level. We express more and more symptoms. What do I mean by putting "holes in the bucket"? I mean doing anything that does not promote health. Doing something that decreases our health is what I mean about putting "holes in the bucket," because holes in the bucket decrease the water level, and the water is the physical thing, like health.

Some common examples of "holes in the bucket" are drinking alcohol, eating sugar, taking drugs (both prescription and over-the-counter), taking street drugs, experiencing stress, putting poisonous chemicals like pesticides, herbicides, and other things into our body from the food we eat, smoking, misperceptions from faulty belief systems, etc. These are just some of the most common ones, doing things that everyone, including you, knows are not good for us. These are some of the things that take away your health or let the health drain out of your body.

Many people in the natural health care field got smart, and figured out that if you get someone to quit doing the thing that is putting holes in their bucket, the water level in the bucket will go up. They found that if you get someone to plug the holes in the bucket, you will get more health. Because the body is always striving to be healthy.

Have you ever cut your finger? Is it still bleeding? No, not unless you just now cut your finger. That healing is your body striving for health, always doing what it can to make you healthier.

Continuing the bucket analogy, health is like rain. It is always slowly raining, and the water level in the bucket is being replaced as a natural expression of the body wanting to be healthy, to heal.

So when you plug the holes in the bucket by stopping what you are doing to put holes in the bucket, the water level goes up. Your health increases.

That is why you have everyone out there saying: "Eat this food…don't eat that one," and if you listened to everyone about what food not to eat, you would never eat. Don't worry, I will address this later, and end all the confusion over the "diet wars."

For the most part, people are either moving the symptoms around by "treating them," putting them lower in the bucket, and just waiting for new symptoms to emerge, or they are plugging the holes in their bucket waiting for the rain to come in, or waiting for time to pass for their health to increase.

Some people treat the symptoms with surgery, some with prescription drugs, some with over-the-counter drugs, some with supplements, some with acupuncture, some with chiropractic, etc. etc. Some even go so far as to change their lifestyle. They stop eating sugar or other things to attempt to plug the holes in their bucket of health.

Up until this point, most people have not even considered anything outside of this paradigm of treating symptoms. They believed that treating symptoms was what you did to help people heal. Whether you treated symptoms naturally, or with drugs and surgery, all there really was to do was to treat symptoms. That is all that just about anyone has ever thought of doing. This is like water to a fish. The myths that are so "true" to us that they are not even questioned, the things that are so far in the background that we don't even think to question whether they are true or not. They just seem to be that true.

What is this thing that is so far in the background that it is not even questioned?

The answer is, treating symptoms and disease. No one has ever done something other then treating symptoms or disease. I mean, what else is there?

You can move the symptoms around in the bucket and plug the holes in the bucket. That is all you can really do. Or is it?

How about putting a hose in the bucket and turning it on? Turn the hose on full force. This will increase the water level in the bucket dramatically. It is not changing something that is wrong or fixing something that is broken. It is doing something that will make a difference.

Adding water to the bucket is what no one has even considered as an option, let alone figured out how to do it. Well, I have done both, and that is what this book will share with you, how to add to your health,

I will share with you the actual how-to in a later chapter. There are some more myths we need to clear up first. We are still dealing with thinking outside the box. The good news for most people is this: There is nothing you "have to" give up. There is nothing you "have to" not do to be healthy. If you are adding health into the bucket quicker than your health is draining out of the bucket, it doesn't matter what else you do. The key is to be adding more health than is leaking out.

Some people have "genetic weaknesses" in their bucket. This is NOT something that is predestined. It is a tendency. It can be expressed or not, depending on you, and what you do.

For example, if "everyone" in your family has diabetes, it means you have a really weak part of the bucket around sugar. You may have to cut down on sugar because, for you and your bucket, you got the luck of the draw, and sugar blows a HUGE hole in your bucket, compared to other people, for whom the part of their bucket that eating sugar is pounding up against is as thick as a bank vault, and sugar does not have that great of an impact on them. Most people are somewhere in the middle. Add enough sugar, and a hole will be put in your bucket. But if you add enough health, it won't matter. You will still be healthy.

This is why some people can smoke all their lives and never get lung cancer, and others smoke one cigarette and get lung cancer in a week. It is, in part, determined by the genetic "tendency" of your "bucket" and how it reacts to the environment that may be beating it up.

Again, symptoms and disease are what is written on the inside of your bucket. When your health gets low, you begin to express symptoms and disease. If you add health to your bucket, your body will heal, and you will express fewer symptoms and disease.

You can treat the symptoms and you can plug the holes in your bucket. There is nothing wrong with this. Or, you can put a hose in your bucket, and turn it on, thus increasing the level of your health.

Now, this bucket example is a little oversimplified. A more realistic example would be the ocean and the shoreline. Written on the shore, in the sand and rock, are the symptoms and disease your genetics predispose you to. Anything that is covered by the ocean, you do not express. Anything not covered by the ocean will express those symptoms and disease.

This is why people can treat symptoms and disease and have their symptoms go away. If you cut out the rock that the symptom is written on, and throw it in the ocean, it will be covered by water, and you will not experience that symptom or disease. But you have done nothing to add to the level of health of the person. You can dig a hole deep into the sand, where some symptoms you were expressing were written, and then water will fill in that area of the beach. I am sure most of you have done this at one point when you were a kid. You went near the water on the beach, and found that if you dug down far enough, you would get to the water level, and there would be water in your hole. Same concept.

When you treat or fix some symptom or disease in your body, although the symptoms or disease may be gone, you have done nothing to improve your health. Health is the thing to be added to. Health is the physical existence. And when you add to the bucket of health, the body naturally heals symptoms and disease.

You do not have to know what is causing the symptom or disease. You do not have to know what the diagnosis is. You do not have to know anything about what is wrong. You can add to your health and your body will heal itself.

Chapter 16

The Reality of Cause, Diagnosis, Treatment, Cure and (Not) Getting Old

I will revisit some things I talked about earlier, because now that you understand what health really is, what I'm telling you makes even more sense.

The first issue is "cause." What is the cause of sickness? Many people pay it lip service, but what is it really? Going with the bucket analogy, what is the cause of one of the symptoms or diseases not being covered by water, or being expressed? Could it be that water is leaking out of the bucket? Which hole, though, is responsible or the "cause" of the symptoms or disease? That is kind of a trick question.

It is not just one hole that causes a symptom or disease. Or, said another way, there is not just one cause to any symptom or disease. In fact, everything you did or didn't do up to that point in your life has some role in the symptoms or disease you are expressing. Most people are looking for a cause, and no one ever stopped to question if there even was only one cause. Until now. The cause, if you really need to have one, is a lack of health.

To get people to immediately stop looking for the one cause that doesn't exist would be tough. Because looking for the cause of something is so engrained into our thinking, into our very way of automatic reaction, that stopping the never-ending quest for "cause" immediately is like expecting a huge semi truck to stop instantly, even though it is going down the highway at 70 miles per hour (120 km/h).

With one little change, two little words, the track that most people head down when looking for the cause would be much more effective. That is, switching one's frame of mind from looking for the cause to looking for the major contributing factors, because some things contribute more to certain symptoms and disease than others. Some contribute more directly, other less directly. Switching to looking for contributing factors instead of the cause will make a quantum leap in how effective the treatment of the symptoms and disease becomes.

That is worth saying again, in BOLD. **There is not one cause to anything. There are infinite amounts of contributing factors, some that are contributing more than others, to the symptoms or disease being expressed.** To look for one cause is to go down a highway looking for a destination that you will never find. The highway doesn't end.

Here is some quick science, for those wanting some proof beyond the common sense reason and logic of it all. The bootstrap theory of quantum physics roughly says that every part of the universe is intimately interconnected with everything else. Every part of the universe knows what every other part of the universe is doing. What this means, translated into English, is that there is not one cause to anything, in the body, or in the universe. For any one thing in the universe to be where it is, every other part of the universe has to be exactly where it is, and everything is a cause for everything else. Some things are more of a contributing factor than others.

I have talked a little about diagnosis with the light and darkness analogy. I also talked about it in Chapter 4. There is a little more that needs to be known about diagnosis. And since it is so important, I will talk about it again.

What is a diagnosis? It is information about a shadow that, when enough light is present, goes away, even if you had no information about the shadow. Diagnosis is a made-up story. It is fabricated. It is a story, made up, imagined, out of thin air, but based on facts. Now, before too many people get all upset about that statement, and before I explain to you that understanding this is important, let me show you what I mean.

What is a headache? It is a pain in the head. What can cause a pain in your head? Lack of water, restricted blood flow, pressure on the brain, a tumor, someone hitting you on the head with a hammer, etc. There are many things that can contribute to your having pain in your head. The problem is that, when you get pain in your head, and it fits certain parameters, the label of "headache" is put on the pain. What is headache? It is a made-up name. It is a word that was created, imagined, and used to describe a pain in the head. It was imagined. The pain in your head is there, and the label, the made-up word, the diagnosis used to describe it, headache, is just that, made up.

Fibromyalgia is an even better example. Fibromyalgia is a made-up label put on you if you have a certain number of symptoms on the list entitled "fibromyalgia," and certain sore spots on your body. Where did this list come from? It was made up. Some of the things on this list are pain, painful spots within the muscles, fatigue, etc. What can contribute to fatigue in a person? Not enough sleep, avoiding some conflict, not getting the proper food to supply the body with energy, and slow metabolism are some possible causes of fatigue. What can contribute to aches and pains in the body? Lack of certain vitamins and minerals can. What can contribute to a lack of vitamins and minerals in the body? Not eating the right foods, the small intestine not absorbing them properly, the body not being able to move the vitamins and minerals across the cell membranes. What can contribute to the small intestine not absorbing them properly? Lack of blood flow and hormone imbalance can. What can contribute to hormone imbalances?

Are you starting to get the picture? Fibromyalgia is a label, a made-up word used to put a label on a person who has enough symptoms on a list that was also made up. That is what I mean when I say that symptoms and especially diseases are made up, fabricated, not real. The physical and mental process behind the label, however, is very real.

It is extremely important to understand this about symptoms and disease, and not just blow it off. Understanding this will help you begin to loosen the grip of the myth that there is "a cause" for "a disease." What is a disease? It is a group of symptoms with a label put on them, and how many contributing factors can any one given symptom have? (If you are not sure, see the above again, where I only talked a little about one symptom.) In fact, according to quantum physics, an infinite amount. Some contributing factors just have more of an effect than others.

What most people do when they get a label is that they then set out to get rid of that label, losing sight of where the label came from. They make the label the "thing," the "entity," the physical thing to be gotten rid of, destroyed, or treated away. They forget the very fact that the label was made up. It does NOT exist. It is NOT real. It is NOT physical. How can you get rid of something that is made up, not real, fictitious, especially if you think it is real?

This reminds me of a story, about a thief who used to break into candy bar machines, and steal the candy bars out of the machine. The police set out to catch this thief. No matter what they did, they could never catch the thief. Finally, after exhausting all of their options, they put up security cameras to catch the thief. And you know what they found? A squirrel. A squirrel was crawling into the machines, getting the candy bars and crawling out. No matter how hard the police tried, they were never going to catch a person stealing the candy bars. The person did not exist. The person was not real.

This is what happens when you try to treat the labels, the diagnosis.

The diagnosis is not what the problem is. It is not what is wrong. It is not as if being given a diagnosis gives you some resolution on the matter. There is none. The diagnosis is in fact usually just a fancy Latin name for the symptoms. It is made up, not real. It is pretty tough to get rid of something that is not real.

For example, "headache" is the common name; "cephalgia" is the Latin diagnosis, and it means "head + pain." Swelling in the knee =

diagnosis of "effusion," which means "swelling." Fibro+myalgia = "muscle pain." On and on. The diagnosis usually does not actually give you any new information that you didn't already know.

If you really want to know what is wrong, what is "causing" your _____ (and put any symptom you want here) is a lack of health, and everything in the universe as it is. There, now don't you feel much better? Yeah, right. If you want to look for major contributing factors in order to eliminate them, go for it. And remember, there is no one cause; there are only major contributing factors. Keeping this in mind will make all the difference in the world.

With this understanding, you will see how utterly ridiculous it is to look for a cure for a disease, because the disease label itself is made up. How do you cure something that is not real? Pretty tough. Looking for one cause, again, is impossible. Medicine has primarily been looking for one cause for every illness, and that is why it has come up empty. The medical symptoms and disease care system has not found the cause for any disease, because the diagnosis does not exist, and you cannot find a cure for something that does not exist.

Again, diagnosis is the shadow, and when you turn on the light, the information about the shadow becomes irrelevant. Diagnosis is made up, and trying to find the one cure for the diagnosis has not worked, mainly because there is not one cause. There are multiple, multiple contributing factors to any given expression of a lack of health, some being symptoms and disease.

Then there is the idea of prevention, but mostly as it lives in the world today, it is a joke. To the medical profession, prevention is vaccinations. For most others, it is taking vitamins and cutting back on the number of times that you do the things that are bad for you. This is what most people do when they talk about prevention. Even less is actually done about prevention. Adding to your health is the first real solution for prevention.

Old age is another great topic that fits here nicely. So many people are afraid of death and old age. In fact, the fear of death is second only to the fear of public speaking. The fear of death is a big issue. I will get rid of any fear of death that might be left, right now.

Why is it that so many people fear death and old age? I will address the old age question first. The proof I gave earlier was the *National Geographic* article that showed people living, on average, to 120-140 years old. And they were as youthful and energetic as 40-year-old people in our culture.

What happens when you get older? Everyone thinks they know that when you get old and decrepit you have to start wearing diapers again, and you need a cane, walker, or wheelchair. You need to depend on other people to feed and take care of you. You lose your freedom. Everyone knows this, right? That is just what happens when you get older. That is actually another myth I will shatter, the myth that old age has to equal losing your health.

So many people believe that getting old is the same thing as losing your health. Some think of the two as the same thing. THEY ARE NOT the same thing. If you have a hole in your bucket and the water is dripping out, what will happen to the water level in the bucket as time passes? That's right, the water level will get lower. As time passes, you will have less and less water in the bucket, because it is dripping out.

Everyone is born into life with a certain level of health. What happens for almost everyone is that they do nothing to add to their level of health. Some do things to plug up the holes in the bucket, or treat the symptom that they cannot tolerate anymore. But most do nothing to add to their level of health.

So what happens as you get older? That is right, your level of health gets lower, and you express more and more symptoms. If you do nothing to add to your health, years pass, and your level of health get lower and lower. Your lack of health leaves you needing a wheelchair, walker, or cane, diapers, and other people to care for you, etc. That is all it is. A lack of health. If you had enough health and were 90 years old, you would still have your freedom and youthfulness. You wouldn't have symptoms or diseases, either.

Old age does not have to mean you are not healthy. If you do nothing to add to your level of health, old age will mean you are not healthy. If you add to your level of health, and add health more quickly than you are losing it, you will have more years of life with no decrease in health. You will remain vital, youthful, energetic, happy, and all the other great things that go along with good health.

You can be old, and completely healthy, as if you were still 40 or 50. All you have to do is add to your health more quickly than you are taking it away.

Chapter 17

Bazuji

Bazuji is a word I invented. I made up. The essence of Bazuji is the full potential of being human, realized on all levels. Since I made up the word, I get to make up the definition, and my definition is *the* definition. If you don't like my definition, make up your own word or use another word.

I made up this word because everyone has their own definition of health and well being, and they think their definition is right. And it is.

This presents a problem. Because when I say "health," you think of the definition you have for health. And you think that your definition is the same thing I am talking about. It is like love. When I say "love," you have your own definition of what love is to you. And when I say "love," you think of your definition, and think that I mean the same thing you are thinking, when, often, I am not.

This is actually a problem many times when using language to communicate. I say a word and it goes through all of your filters and definitions of what that particular word means to you, and then you assume that what I meant is what your definition is when, often, it isn't.

I created my own word with my own definition of what it is, so that when I use this word in the future, you will know exactly what I am talking about, almost. See, the words that make up the definition create the same problem. When I say "you," many people think of different things. So part of this chapter will be about the definition and what the essence of it means, behind everyone's filters and ideas.

Bazuji (pronounced "bay – ZOO – jee," with the accent on the **zu**):
1. You and your being (Body/Mind/Spirit)— perfect, connected as one, fully expressing the perfection
2. "I AM" perfectly expressed

In its truest essence, Bazuji is a verb. It is a continual process, happening now, though most often it will be used as a noun. *Bazuji* is what I am being.

It can also be an adjective. I am *bazuji*.

An adverb is made by adding "ly." I *bazujily* honor God

What does this definition mean?

It means "you and your being." This means all parts of you, everything about you. The way you think. The relationships you are in. Your moods, emotions, and thoughts. Your chemistry. All the organs and the endocrine system. The muscles and bones and ligaments. All of your systems—the immune system, endocrine system, circulatory system, all of them. Your conscious thoughts and subconscious thoughts. Your spirit and the life force that is giving you life. The intelligence governing everything about you. This includes everything you know about you, and even the things you don't know about who you are. This is the full scope of "you" I am talking about.

"Perfect". This means everything about you working perfectly. Your moods are always exactly what you want. Your relationships are perfect. Your organs are functioning perfectly. Your endocrines and hormone balance working perfectly. Your thoughts are adapting and responding to the environment. The experience of stress is completely gone because the parts of you, that respond and react to stress, are working perfectly. Therefore you handle and deal with the stress, perfectly, and you experience nothing, no stress. The parts of you that deal with the experience of the outside world are, working perfectly, leaving you feeling peaceful and content at all times. The parts of you that deal with healing symptoms and disease are working perfectly, so you will have no symptoms or disease. Your emotions are an expression of how you feel, working perfectly, neither governing nor controlling you, not being there when you don't want them. Your emotions become an experience, and your body then handles them and the emotions going away. Your experience of the world is perfect. You always make the choices that are perfect. You do what you want to do all the time. Everything about you, your mind, thoughts, body, feelings, spirit, and inner wisdom are all working perfectly. As they work perfectly, the world around you will be working exactly the way you want it to.

"Connected as one." This refers to the whole of you, everything about you, working as one cohesive unit. This is best described with an example.

If you can, imagine a government that doesn't work as a team, where all the parts are not working together. They are not communicating, and most do not know what the others are doing. I know it is probably tough to imagine, but try.

Now, imagine if the different parts of government actually worked together, if everyone knew what everyone else was doing. If they all knew what was going on, and worked as a team towards a common goal, in the same direction, without fighting or conflict, what would be possible?

This is what I mean when I say "connected as one." All the different parts of you are one synchronized whole, working together towards the goal of *bazuji* and what you want. Your thoughts, body and spirit are all aligned, going in the same direction, connected as one. Imagine what would be possible. The possibilities would be essentially limitless.

"Fully expressing." This is an active process, constantly happening now.

It is not just the potential of perfection, or the potential of the synchronicity happening between all aspects of you. It is all of that happening now. All of everything being present now, as an experience and as results. Because it is one thing to actually have all that without actually expressing it, and another to actually express and experience it all now.

"Perfection." This is the same perfection I talked about earlier, but expressed. Tangible results happen, results of the perfection manifest.

This is *bazuji*, you and your being (Body/Mind/Spirit), perfect, connected as one, fully expressing the perfection.

This is my target, the target of what I want to be. I talked earlier about getting a target. This is my suggestion for what you can make your target for health and well being. You can change it, add to it, or do whatever you want to it. But if it is not this, it is something other than *bazuji*.

Now, just having a target does not guarantee that you will hit your target. But before you have the urge to give up, let me ask you this: If you keep shooting at the same target over and over and over and over and over again, what do you think the odds are that you will eventually hit the target? Pretty good. In fact, given long enough, I would say there is a 100% chance you will eventually hit the target.

So having the target does not guarantee *bazuji*. But constantly going for it, over and over again, 100% guarantees you will eventually hit it. This is not to mention all the invaluable experience and knowledge you will attain along the way.

Bazuji is a suggested target, but you can have any target you want, and you can change it later if you want. So go ahead, take a moment now and find your target. Create or modify your existing target if you want.

Actually take the time to do it right now. It might be as simple as saying, "I want *bazuji* as my target." Or you can create your own target. But do it. Now. And keep going for this target. Keep focused on this target. Play with it, the way a child plays at something new that they are learning, not like an adult, who tries it once and, if it doesn't work, they give up.

Now this is key. Keep focused on the target. Because, as we all know, if you are riding a bike and there is a big rock up ahead, and you keep saying to yourself "I am not going to hit the rock, I am not going to hit the rock, I am not going to hit the rock," what do you do? You hit the rock. Because that is what you were focused on. If you focus on the path around the rock, where you are going, and keep focused on that, you are much more likely to go along that path and avoid the rock.

In the same way, if you are focused on not having headaches, or not having pain, or not having cancer, what do you think you will likely end up with? That thing you are focusing on not having. If you focus on getting rid of cancer, you will probably end up with more cancer. If you are focused on getting rid of the headaches you experience, you will probably still have headaches. It is like the rock. You need to focus on what you want, where you are going, not on what you are trying to get rid of.

So, a word of caution: When creating your target, make sure it is a target of what you want, not what you don't want. For example, if you have headaches and don't want them, think of what would it be like if they were gone. How would you feel, what would be happening, what would your moods and energy levels be like? Put what everything would be like, what you want, into your target.

To me it is amazing that, with almost everyone in the medical symptoms and disease care system focused on what they are trying to get rid of, and focused on the symptoms and disease, that anyone actually heals. Almost everyone focuses on the thing you don't want, the symptoms or disease you don't want, yet some people actually heal. This, to me, is an amazing tribute to the inborn wisdom that guides and runs our body.

So find a target, if you don't already have one.

Section two review

- Who you are being is the key to your *bazuji* and your life
- Health is the thing that you must add to
- There is no one cause, one cure. There are many contributing factors to every symptom or disease, and the contributing factors are different for everyone
- Diagnosis is a made-up label that doesn't exist, and you cannot treat and get rid of something that is made up, because it is not real
- Diagnosis is a label picked off the top of a list of a bunch of symptoms someone has, and the cause of all these symptoms is different in everyone. Therefore, there will never be one cure for   any disease
- Bazuji is: 1. You and your being (Body/Mind/Spirit)—perfect, connected as one, fully expressing the perfection 2. "I AM" perfectly expressed.

SECTION THREE

Who You Can Be and
What You Can Do

Chapter 18

Follow Your Inner Knowing

This is the chapter that I consider to be the most important of all the chapters in this book. This is the chapter that I invite you to read more than once. Read this chapter again, and you will begin to understand where a lot of the information in this book came from. Everything else in this book is great at helping to shift your thinking, and get you to be the person you need to be to get what you want. This chapter, however, will far surpass the rest of the book added together, not in terms of intellectual understanding, but in an experiential, physical, real difference way, in a *your life* type of way.

You will not get some great understanding or profound wisdom from this chapter. What you will get, from applying what is in this chapter, is great understandings and profound wisdom over and over again. When you shift your being with this chapter, and express that new way of being, the world will come alive for you.

I want to share a small, but hugely profound insight. It is in the form of a question and an experience most of us can relate to. You are going through life, and you figure out what you need to do. You have weighed all the pros and cons, and you know what there is to do. You have done this with your mind, thinking. Then you are about to do what you have decided to do, and you have this knowing or feeling to do something else. Some people call this their intuition, or a gut feeling, which is different than emotions. But you have this knowing that doesn't seem to make any sense based on the information that you had, so you decide to go with your original decision. Then you look back, and what do you do? You wish you had trusted your gut. You wish you had followed your intuition.

You followed what made logical sense in your mind, but you wish you had listened to that inner wisdom that told you otherwise. And, in looking back, you realize that that inner wisdom was right. It would have been better to do what your inner knowing said, even though, at the time, it didn't make any sense, even though, at the time, the inner knowing did not seem to be an appropriate choice.

How many times have you done this? How many times have you "hit yourself on your head" for not listening to this knowing? If you are like most people, too many times to count. Or at least, often. You had a knowing to do something different. You didn't listen, and did what made sense in your mind, and then you looked back and regretted it.

This is not new; most people know this. They say it to themselves every time they do it. *Why did I do that again? I knew better.* And then they do it again at some point in the future. Knowing this has not really made a difference in the past.

Have you ever done this? It is the opposite of the scenario above. How many times have you weighed all the pros and cons, come up with a decision you thought was best, got a knowing, intuition, or gut feeling, and knew you should do something else. You then followed this inner knowing. And when you looked back, you were so glad you did. You didn't know why at the time, but ultimately things turned out so much better than if you had gone with your original choice. That "knowing" you had was right, a couple of times, multiple times, maybe lots of times, for some.

I have another question for you that most people never ask, or even consider. This question, when you remember the answer, will make a difference for you in who you are being. The answer will help you to actually listen to this inner knowing in situations you face in the future.

The real question uses the same scenario as above, with a different outcome. I bet you have NEVER done this. How many times have you weighed the pros and cons, come up with a decision about what you are going to do, then received a knowing about something different. You listened to that inner knowing and followed it. You did what the inner knowing guided you to do. But then you looked back and wished you had not. You wish you had listened to your mind, to your original thought process. Have you ever done this? Have you ever, even once in your life, listened to your inner knowing, your gut, over your mind, and regretted it? I bet you never have.

Now, this is really interesting. You have often listened to your mind over your inner knowing, and regretted it. You have listened to your inner knowing and were thankful that you did. And you have NEVER listened to your inner wisdom and regretted it. EVER. What do you want to do more of?

When I realized this, it became really easy for me to trust my inner wisdom and do what it was telling me, even when it didn't make sense. It also actually got me into the habit of asking my inner knowing what to do, and listening to it more than just when it spoke up really loud.

I want to point out a difference here. There is a difference between emotions and the inner knowing. Emotions are the things that you feel, like sadness, anger, joy, happiness, grief, etc. They are things you feel, pure feeling of an experience that can be described. These are emotions. Emotions happen as a response to our thoughts and experiences in life.

The inner knowing is different from emotions. You can access this inner knowing yourself. No one can take it away from you. It is always there when you want it. When you ask your inner knowing what to do, it makes life so incredibly easy. All those really tough decisions in life are gone. All the decisions you make are now simple.

Imagine for a moment going through life and you have to make a decision, a choice about what to do in a particular situation. In the past, this would have been a really difficult choice, and it would have taken you tons of mental energy to think about it. The decision would have taken up days of your life before you could decide what to do. But now, this time, you make the choice within hours, and you know it is the best choice. You trust in the choice, and are at ease with making it, whereas in the past, you would have been concerned, and thinking about the choice, even after you made it.

Imagine all your choices in life being that easy. You would be calmer. You would have more time. You would be less stressed. Because all the tough decisions that need to be made would no longer be tough. That is a glimpse of what is available for you from this chapter.

In case you missed it, I call this your inner knowing, the knowing of what is best for you, based on everything in the universe, not just the limited intellect.

I want to go back to something similar I asked you before, but a little differently this time. Of everything there is to know about everything that is happening, and will be happening, and could be happening on this planet, how much does any one individual know? Of everything there is to know, how much do you know? Less than 1%, I would say.

Now imagine you were going to have your taxes done. And the accountant told you he knew less than 1% about the tax law and your situation. What would you do? You would go somewhere else to get your taxes done. If you were going to go to someone for guidance in your life, and this person knew less than 1% about your situation, would you do what they told you to do?

Well, my friends, that person is you. You just admitted you know less than 1% of everything there is to know about what is going on in this world. Your conscious mind, that is, knows less than 1% of what there is to know. Yet you rely on that limited knowledge to make your choices about life. You are asking someone for recommendations who knows less than 1% about the situation, and you are listening to their recommendations. That is what you are doing.

Up until now, this was your best option. Up until now, following your mind and thoughts and the limited knowledge of what they knew, was the best option. It was the best you knew how to do.

I am now giving you another option, a choice that you may not have known even existed before. That is the choice of listening to your inner knowing. This inner knowing is the knowledge you get from inside yourself, that comes from something greater than you, That comes from something that knows much more than just 1% about what is happening. This inner knowing knows 100% about what is happening.

The psychologist Carl Jung called this the Collective Unconscious. He described this as a pool of thought and ideas. It is almost as if what one person knows is put into this "collective unconscious," and the subconscious mind has access to this information. This collective unconscious is what the subconscious mind actually uses to help run the body.

I have referred to the inner knowing before. It is the knowing that comes through the heart brain. The inner wisdom is similar to the subconscious mind, in that it knows everything there is to know about running the body and mind. It has access to the "perfect blueprint of health," if you will. This is the wisdom that created you from an egg and a sperm. This inner knowing is also a connection to your Creator. It is one of the ways in which God can communicate with you.

The physiology behind this inner knowing is the "heart brain center" I referred to earlier. Joseph Chilton Pierce, in his book *Biology of Transcendence*, does an amazing job of describing the anatomy and physiology of this inner knowing and how it evolved.

Some of you might be saying to yourselves: *What is this inner knowing he is talking about? I have not ever gotten a gut feeling, or really had an intuition. How can I get this? How can I develop this inner knowing to be clear, reliable, and how can I trust it more?* Here is how:

The inner knowing is not an experience in response to the environment or our thoughts. It is something that happens before our thoughts and experiences. The inner knowing can "speak" to people in different ways.

One of the ways this inner knowing speaks to you is like the knowing you get when you are full and know you should stop eating. Another way the inner knowing speaks to you is through symptoms, but you only get symptoms if you don't listen to your inner knowing sooner.

For me, the inner knowing is just that, a knowing. And there is a sensation that happens around my heart. I would not call it a feeling. It almost feels as if someone is holding my heart with their hand and moves my heart in different ways. This different movement brings me my knowing of yes and no, and all the other shades of grey in between.

For others, it is their gut feeling. They just know. Everyone is a little different, and if you go through the steps below, you will know how your inner knowing communicates with you.

So, are you ready? Here is one of those things you can do. And, as I have asked and recommended, do this. Of all the things in this book I have suggested that you do, I feel this is the most important.

Focus on your heart. Right now, shift your awareness to your heart. Feel what your heart feels like right now. Bring your attention to a time when you felt the most love, when you felt the most open and free, the time that brought you the most joy. You got it? If not, take a moment and remember that moment. Actually get present to that moment. When you have your attention on that moment, feel what your heart feels like right now. This is your inner knowing speaking to you, your inner knowing getting your attention and saying "yes."

Now, think about something else. Then focus on your heart and feel what your heart feels like. This is your inner wisdom when it is saying "no."

That is how your inner knowing communicates with you. Don't worry if you are not 100% sure about the difference right now. The more you listen or even try to listen to your inner knowing, the stronger and clearer the response will be, just as the more you use your muscles, the stronger they will be.

Your inner knowing can speak to you in more than yes and no. It can speak full ideas and thoughts to you as well, because of the direct connection your heart brain has with your brain.

All you have to do is focus on your heart center, ask, and the knowing of what to do will come. Now act. Act immediately. Do not hesitate. Follow and take action on what your inner knowing says.

When I say "ask," I mean you can ask anything. Ask about a decision you have to make. Ask about what to do. You can ask about some new supplement or healing modality. You can ask about what food to buy at the grocery store and what food to order at a restaurant. You can ask about any choice or decision you have to make. Ask about everything. You can even ask about the things you wouldn't think there was anything to ask about. Then, take action on what your inner knowing is telling you.

To take it even one step further, just let this inner knowing speak to you whenever it wants. Be open for what your inner knowing has to say. Remember earlier, when you were imagining that moment when you felt the most love? That is what the inner knowing will do when it wants to talk to you. Listen to what it has to say, and act. Act immediately on what it has to say.

In times when you feel stressed, or there is a decision you are having a hard time making, or anytime you are experiencing anything other than peace and freedom within is a great time to specifically pay attention to your inner knowing and ask for guidance.

It is with this inner knowing that you will have 100% confidence in every choice you make. It may not make sense at the time, but you will be sure it is right. This inner knowing will help you know what to do with any new information that comes your way. This inner knowing is what will always tell you what is best for you and your family. This inner knowing will tell you what is right for you, always.

This inner knowing is the key to the kingdom within. Follow this inner knowing and it will never lead you astray. Follow this inner knowing and you will be peaceful and free at all times.

Chapter 19

You Must Know Your Target

I did the bow and arrow example with you earlier. If you need to review why you need to know the target, go back and do that now.

You need to know your target if you expect to hit it. If you have no interest in getting what you want, then knowing your target is not essential.

Many of us, probably even you, want this thing called health, yet have no idea what it would look like if we had it. We are going after this elusive thing, but we really have never stopped to think about what it was. We have never thought about what having *bazuji* would be like, what our world would be like.

Now is the time to do that. Figure out the target for how much *bazuji* you want. You can choose my target of *bazuji*, or you can come up with your own target. If you chose my target, it makes the rest of this chapter really easy. If you want to create your own target, there are some things we need to do first. To do that, we need to lay the groundwork, create the foundation for you to figure out what you want. You can also use these recommendations to create targets in other areas of your life as well.

First, there is no right answer. There is no one way that everybody must be. There is not even a target you must keep forever. The beauty of creating a target for *bazuji* is that you get to say. You get to make it up. You get to create what you want it to look like. And whatever you create, you can change it later if you want to. You can create something different. You get to have whatever you want for a target. So as I go through this, don't worry about being right. Focus on going for whatever you want, because you can always change your mind later.

In creating what you would like for a target of *bazuji*, there are some guidelines to follow that will make them easier. You are creating a picture, an outcome of what it will actually look like when you reach your target, what it will feel like, be like, and all the details about what will happen when you reach your target. You can think of it like this: You are creating a short movie, or picture, representing what the target being reached would look like. You want to paint as many details of this picture as possible.

Let me give you an example from one of my targets.

It is June 10, 2005. I am living from my heart center, in worship of the "I AM" presence, completely following my inner knowing, being *bazuji*. I have met, live with, and am involved with my ideal woman and partner in life. She is lying there in bed now, as I give gratitude for everything, everything that the "I AM" is creating.

My inner knowing is fully alive and expressing its perfection. I fall in love with my partner every day, and make her fall in love with me every day. I can feel my body vibrating. I can see myself in the mirror looking exactly the way I want to look. I can feel my energy; I am full of vitality.

My ideal woman and I are developing our relationship, while being deeply and profoundly in love. I can smell her sweet, wonderful, beautiful, natural fragrance; I love it. I can feel her smooth skin, her hair, her face so sweet, soft, and silky. All of her. I can taste her succulent lips. Her ravishing and gorgeous beauty takes my breath away every day.

Everyone is smiling, happy, and is winning in their situations, interactions, and encounters with us.

This is an example of some of my goals. This is what it will be like when I reached them.

What I use to help create these targets is what I call SMARTS targets SMARTS stands for:

Simple, Sensory, and Specific

Measurable and Meaningful

As If Now

Realistic

Time Framed

Smiley Factor

Some more about what these all mean:

"S": Simple is exactly that. Simple. Do not make it too complicated, or long and drawn out. Most people should be able to understand what it is. If it is a goal around some specific field, most of your colleagues should be able to understand your target.

"S": Sensory involves all of your senses. You use your sense of vision. You hear things in this picture and movie. You smell things in your movie of your target. You feel things, both with your hands and with your emotions. In your picture, you have the internal voice in your head that you always have. You put all of these different senses into your picture, as well as the most important one, the inner knowing of your heart brain. Make sure to get that in the picture or movie as well.

"S": Specific. This is best illustrated with an example. I have moved many times in my life. Every time I moved, I created a list of what I want. And every time there was a fireplace on that list. The first time, I was looking at a place that had everything I wanted but a fireplace. I mentioned this to the landlord and she laughed. She took me into the unfinished basement, and there was a plastic fireplace in the basement. I learned from this, and when I was looking for the next place I put a real fireplace on my list. I found a place that had everything except a fireplace. I said this to the landlord and he said that there was a fireplace. It was just boarded up behind the wall. The next place I moved into, I put a real working fireplace on the list of what I wanted. I found a place with a real working fireplace this time, but the landlord would not let me use it. So finally I put on my list "a real working fireplace I can use." And the next time, I got it. You need to be specific.

"M": Measurable. There must be some specific way in which you measure the results, a quantifiable way that you know the goal is achieved.

"M": Meaningful. The target, the goal must be meaningful to you. It must be something you want and desire. If it means nothing to you, there will be no reason to keep going for it. It does not work to have it be something that someone else wants for you.

"A": As If Now. Write your movie in the present tense, as if you are describing a situation that is happening now. Tomorrow never comes. It is like the sign "Free money tomorrow." You come back the next day and the sign still says, "Free money tomorrow." Tomorrow never comes. If you write your goals in the future, the future never comes.

"R": Realistic. Your target must be believable to you. If you do not think you can attain it, chances are you probably will not attain it. Now, this means two things. One, if you have a faulty belief system about what you can and cannot do and you want to change it, you might want to try my CDs. Two, "realistic" is different for everyone. For some, making a million dollars in one year is totally attainable. For others, it is not. Make sure your target is realistic to you.

"T": Time Framed. Put a definite date on your target. Put the date as if today is the date, and write your goal with that date now. This is similar to As If Now, but with an actual date or time frame.

"S": Smiley Factor. Make sure that you are smiling and happy in the picture, that your goal includes your being happy. Here is an example of why: You have a goal to be in Italy within five years, but no smiley factor. You get some rare cancer that the only know treatment for is in Italy, and you have to fly there to get your cancer treated. This is not what you want.

Make sure you do not have negatives in your goals. It is not good to say something like "no more pain," because remember, what you focus on is what you get. So if you are focusing on "no pain", "pain" is actually what you are focusing on. If you don't want this or that, you have to put it in your target as a positive. Like if the pain were gone, what would be there? You might be feeling great, or have free movement in your neck or whatever. Just make sure you put all the things you don't want in terms of what you would have when they were gone, so you can focus on what you want, because that is what you will get.

You then must envision this and ask for it. Demand that the Creator provide this to you. The Creator wants to give you abundance, wants to give you what you want. All you have to do is create the goal, envision it, and focus on it. Put in feeling and make it real.

So if you want my target, take it. If you want to add to my target, do so. If you want to change it, do that. Just create your target. If you want *bazuji* as your target, great. Create your target(s).

Chapter 20

Seven Things That Add to Your Level of Bazuji

Finally, there are things you can actually do, and these things are what you would naturally do if you were *bazuji*. You would find yourself doing this if you listened to your inner knowing. I am listing them because it helps shorten the learning curve.

They are all simple and easy, most of them are free, and if you do these things, you are guaranteed to see improvements and changes in your level of *bazuji*.

Each one of these is something everyone can do. Each one of these is so incredibly simple they almost seem too simple. The key is who you have to be to do these things.

Here they are:

1. Communication - Listening, Acting and Requesting
2. Rest - Physically and Mentally
3. Breathing Fresh Air
4. Food and Water - Quality and Quantity
5. Sunlight
6. Activity - Physical and Mental
7. Consciousness

It is my stand, my belief, that when you do these things, you will be well. You will be *bazuji*. If you do all of these things to the full scope of what they are, you will have *bazuji*. You will not have to worry about whether you should go to a medical symptoms and disease care doctor, because you will not have any symptoms or disease. It really is that simple.

Your body, your being is a glorious machine. It has the wisdom to heal itself, if you just listen to what it is saying. If you just give your body what it wants, if you listen and do what your body wants, you will be *bazuji*. It really is that simple.

If you want to pretend it is more complicated, if you want to think that there is more to health than that, go ahead. Be my guest. When you live and play in the world of treating symptoms and disease, when you try to find the one cause to find the one cure, that world is really complicated. But remember, your beliefs are what create your reality. So why not choose beliefs that are easy and empower you?

What I am sharing with you is a whole new perspective from which to view your life and *bazuji*. When you view and approach life in this way, it really is simple.

So let's go into these seven things and the full scope of what they mean.

Communication

Communication means having communication present in all areas of your life. The most important area of communication for *bazuji* is between you and your inner knowing. This is the same inner knowing I talked about earlier, in Chapter 18. This inner knowing is constantly communicating to you. This inner knowing is constantly sharing with you what it wants. It is just a matter of listening to it and, more importantly, acting on what it says. That is what a lot of Chapter 18 was about, listening and taking action on what this inner knowing is communicating to you.

That, right there, is the biggest gold mine of not only being *bazuji*, but of your life. So I think I will say it again.

Your inner knowing is always communicating with you. And if you simply take action on what it says, you will have *bazuji*. You will also end up with the exact life you truly want.

This inner knowing is your spirit, or the essence of what is breathing life into you. It is the Creator's presence, guiding you. If you will, it is God communicating with you.

Communication also means between all the different parts of your body. I will let you in on a little secret. The key to your *bazuji* is communication, all the different organs, endocrine glands and every other thing and process communicating, working as a team to keep you *bazuji*.

It is like the example of the government I gave earlier. If all the different parts of the government work together and communicate with each other, anything is possible. The same thing is true in your body. If the individual parts are not communicating, your health and *bazuji* will not be as good as they could be. You will not be expressing your full potential in life. If all your parts are communicating and working together, you will be much more *bazuji*. It would be impossible not to be *bazuji* if everything were communicating in your body.

This type of communication is actually the missing key to your health, the key that so many people have been looking for. Let me explain.

You almost never have a problem with any of the individual parts of your body. All the parts of your body almost always know exactly what to do. Always. The problem is, they often don't get the message. Your brain says "Hey, liver, detoxify the blood." What the liver hears is static and it doesn't get the message. So then the liver sits there and does nothing. The body remains toxic. Or the liver tells the pancreas, "Hey, pancreas, we need more insulin." And the pancreas says, "What? What did you say?" And the pancreas then sits around doing nothing while the diabetic's blood sugar levels go through the roof. Or the stomach is told to release digestive enzymes, doesn't get the message, and you get heartburn and indigestion. It is almost never the individual part that doesn't know what to do. It simply doesn't get, or ignores, the messages.

If the communication of messages among all the sites in your body is working effectively, your body is a synchronized whole, working together to produce *bazuji* for you.

Your lack of *bazuji* almost always results because the messages among all the parts are not getting through. The communication is not happening. So when the communication starts happening, you will start healing automatically, naturally, through the powers that created you, often without having to treat this, that, or that other thing, because they heal naturally.

The great part about this type of communication is this: If you listen to your inner knowing and act on what it says, you will automatically have all the parts of your body communicating. If you listen, your parts will follow suit and begin listening and acting on what is told to them.

There is also another great way I know of to help speed up all your parts communicating. It is The BodyTalk System.™ Basically, The BodyTalk System™ uses your body's inner wisdom to figure out what your body wants to do, and then does it. What The BodyTalk System™ usually ends up doing is restoring communication within your body. It is amazing. If you are at all interested, check out their website at www.bodytalksystem.com.

There are other systems that help restore communication between all the different places in your being. Many of them do this by removing barriers to that communication. Stored emotions are one of the most common blocks to this communication. Time Line Therapy™ is one of the most effective and simple ways of removing emotional blocks. It also helps you remove and change faulty belief systems that can be getting in the way of this communication. You can check out their website at www.timelinetherapy.com or the CD sets I talked about earlier do the same thing for you as well.

Chiropractic is another great way to restore communication. Contrary to popular opinion, chiropractic offers way more than just the treatment of back and neck pain. Chiropractic helps restore this communication between all the different parts of the body, so the body can work as a whole.

Chiropractic is very simply this: Your nerves control your moods, emotions, actions, energy levels, sleep, thinking, digestion, pain, muscles, organs, endocrine glands, hearing, vision, eyes, skin, bones, immune system, and everything else in your body. Your nerves also control everything that makes you who you are. Chiropractic allows your nerves to work better. Therefore, everything you do, everything your body does, and who you are, can improve with chiropractic care.

All the confusion comes because there are so many different types of chiropractic. Most people, including many chiropractors, try to lump all chiropractors into one group. Chiropractors are similar to medical doctors in respect to all the different specialties there are within chiropractic. Chiropractors specialize in all sorts of areas like; sports medicine, athletes, wellness care, vitalism, back pain, neck pain, allergies, nutrition, headaches, kids, people with more years of experience, symptom and disease care, emotional work, spiritual, and just about every type of area that you could imagine.

The specialties of chiropractic that deals with restoring communication within the body are the vitalists, wellness care, and spiritual chiropractors. All specialties of chiropractic are going to restore communication within the body to some extent. Wellness care, spiritual and vitalistic chiropractors just specialize in restoring this communication. They specialize in giving the body back the power to heal itself, by having this communication present.

The biggest form of communication necessary is you communicating with your Creator. Some call this prayer. Others call it visualizing. Others call it meditation. Others call it asking or declaring, and yet others call it commanding. My favorite is listening to your inner knowing. There are probably a couple of others as well. To me they are all the same thing. I do not think the power that created this universe is limited in how thy can hear us communicating to thy. (I like the word thy here, because it is non-gender based, which I believe the Creator is). The Creator can hear your words and thoughts and see your actions and the pictures you create or visualize, and feel what you feel.

To me, communication with your Creator is not something you have to consciously do, because you are always doing it. Everything you think, everything you say, everything you do and everything you picture is a message directly to the Creator and a request, a request to the Creator to co-create with you that which was "asked" for. Because even before you ask, shall you receive. It is a matter of being aware of what you are asking through your thoughts, words, actions, feelings, and visualizations, to be aware at all times of what you are asking for. Not to ask for things you don't want, which you often do inadvertently, having thoughts or saying things that are not for what you want, but by only keeping and having what you want on your mind, in your actions in your words or feelings.

The key in being *bazuji* is this act of asking or commanding, always, exactly what you want, and nothing else, and listening to the Creator answering you through your inner knowing. The powers of the Creator want to give you everything, want to give you exactly what you ask for. If you keep asking for contradicting things, you will have contradicting results in your life.

The powers that created this universe are not limited. The powers of the Creator are unlimited. They can do anything. The only thing that limits them is you. If you get out of the way and open up communication, the powers that be will provide.

Keep the lines of communication open. Listen to what your inner knowing is saying to you. Act on what it is saying, request exactly and only what you want, and you will get it.

1. Communication - Listening, Acting and Requesting
2. Rest - Physically and Mentally
3. Breathing Fresh Air
4. Food and Water - Quality and Quantity
5. Sunlight
6. Activity - Physical and Mental
7. Consciousness

Rest

This means both physical and mental rest. I have to say here, technically, that breathing fresh air is more important than rest, but most of us breathe whether we want to or not, so I put that third. I will get into that next, but for now, back to rest.

I will show you some different ways you can rest. You do not have to do all of them. In fact, you do not have to do any of them. You can do anything you want that is resting. I am just giving you some suggestions that you might be able to use. If one of them works, great. Most things rest both the mind and the body at the same time. If they do, great. If not, you need to also make sure that you rest the other aspect that did not get rest.

Now, when I say "rest," I do not necessarily mean sleep. I think most of us can relate to this experience: You go to sleep at night, and when you wake up in the morning, you are more tired than when you went to sleep at night. If you cannot relate, you can probably at least understand intellectually what I mean. Just because you are sleeping does NOT mean you get rest. Sleeping can equal rest, but it does not automatically equal rest.

So how do you get rest? Well, there are actually many different ways to get rest. One of the simplest is clearing your mind before you go to bed at night. If you fall asleep with a clear mind, your sleep will be more restful. If you go to sleep with all this or any other stuff racing through your mind, your sleep will turn into more of the same, and you will wake up having not rested. Clear your mind before you go to sleep, and you will wake up having rested. You will be refreshed and ready to take on the day physically and mentally.

The best example of how not resting causes problems is the way kids behave. Anyone who has ever been around kids before and after a nap knows exactly how much of a difference rest makes. The kids will whine, cry and be naughty, all just because they are tired. They need to rest. Then they rest, wake up, and they are like new kids again. Not getting enough rest impacts the way we think. Not being rested influences the bad choices we make. Not having enough rest keeps us from being our full potential in all areas of our lives.

Another really great example of not getting enough rest is people who work in manufacturing plants. In the old days, people used to work eight-hour shifts, 12-hour shifts, even 16-hour shifts straight through. They had no lunch, no breaks, nothing. Then someone realized that if they give the workers a break, their overall productivity would go up. That is, if they work 7.5, because they were able to rest for half an hour, they actually produced more than if the worked eight hours straight through. Working less and resting actually produces more than constantly working. Without rest, your productivity goes down. Said another way, without resting, it seems as if you have less time, because you do not get as much done in the same amount of time. So if you are feeling really crunched for time, that is when you need to make sure you rest.

Everyone is different, so there is no set time for how much you should rest. I say: Listen to your inner knowing, and rest as much and as often as it tells you to.

What else counts as rest? Meditation can count as rest. Meditation can also achieve many other things, but rest is definitely one benefit. Often people who meditate before they go to bed at night sleep much better. They get more rest. Sleep doubles the effects of meditating, if for nothing more than clearing the mind before you sleep.

Another great way to get rest is to sit down and do nothing. In the middle of the day, sit down and rest. Do nothing. Relax. You can also do this in the middle of the morning, or the evening, or anytime. You can even lie down and do nothing. Don't think, don't plan your day, and don't watch TV. Just do nothing. This, for many people, is really hard to do. If it is, try one of the other suggestions.

Rest is so important. Even God rested on the seventh day, so one book says. In my opinion, you do not have to rest on Sunday, but you have to rest. One day a week, rest. Rest is rejuvenating and helps you get even more done than if you were to work seven days a week.

1. Communication - Listening, Acting and Requesting
2. Rest - Physically and Mentally
3. Breathing Fresh Air
4. Food and Water - Quality and Quantity

5. Sunlight
6. Activity - Physical and Mental
7. Consciousness

Breathing

Breathing full breaths of fresh air is so important for so many reasons. The most obvious is, if you don't breath, you die really quickly. Now for the less obvious ones.

Fresh Air

In America, the best source of fresh air is outside. The indoor air quality is horrible. In fact, it is usually toxic. Once you begin to know some of the things manufacturers put in household products, you begin to see why. The most obvious one is paint. Even when the smell is gone, the toxicity is not. The paint is still "leaking" toxic fumes into the air for years after it is applied. This is not to mention the older paint with lead in it. The lead in older paint can become airborne just by rubbing the paint. The amount of lead in a quarter-size chip of lead based paint is enough to warrant chelation therapy to remove the lead from a child's body.

That new carpet smell? Formaldehyde. And depending on what chemicals were used to put the carpet in, those usually are additional toxic chemicals. Even when the smell of the carpet goes away, the carpet still "leaks" other chemicals into the air for years to come. Furniture, same thing. Then let's get into the cleaning chemicals that most people use. I won't even go into how toxic they are for the environment. But read the label in regards to their effect on you and your family's bodies. The stuff is toxic. And the list goes on and on. Indoor air quality in America sucks. You need to be outside to get fresh air.

There is one easy solution to this. It is an air cleaner I found. It is the best and, in my opinion, the only air cleaner that actually creates indoor air quality cleaner than outside. Other air cleaners may make the air cleaner than before, but not as fresh as outdoors. This air cleaner, which makes the air fresher than outside, can be found on my website, along with anything else I recommend.

There are degrees of clean air outside. Obviously, the air in the middle of a forest in Montana will be cleaner than the air outside in Chicago. But I promise you, the air quality outside in Chicago is better than any indoor air that does not have a great air purifier.

You need fresh air because of the oxygen in the air. That is pretty obvious as well. Without oxygen, no cell in your body can function. Without oxygen, you die. Well, if you do not get enough oxygen to the cells of your body, they are not going to work as well. That includes your brain cells for thinking. That includes your thyroid gland for energy. That includes your pituitary gland for hormone balance and your moods and emotions, and everything else you can think of.

Full Breaths

Full breaths are also needed partly in order to obtain enough oxygen. With full, big, deep breaths of air, you get more oxygen into your system. Just as when you take quick big breaths, you feel light-headed because of all the oxygen. When you take full big breaths of air, you get more oxygen into your system.

This is also important for three other known reasons. First is lymphatic movement. The lymph system is like the sewer system of your body. And without full breaths, the sewer system of your body is not moving. Imagine, as ugly as it is, a city where the sewer system does not move, where the sewer system is backed up everywhere. How well would things in that city work? Not very well. Would you want to live in that city? No way.

It is the same thing in your body. The lymph moves when you breathe with diaphragm movement. The diaphragm is the muscle that moves air in and out of your lungs. The diaphragm acts like the pump in a sewer system, so that everything in your body is working properly and you want to live in your body.

Your diaphragm's movement also moves the fluid around your brain and spinal cord. The fluid is what brings nutrients to your brain and spinal cord, and what brings waste products away from the brain and spinal cord. Do you know everything that the brain and spinal cord control? That is right, everything. So if the brain and spinal cord are not getting what they need, they will not work very well. And if they brain and spinal cord are not working very well, guess what could go wrong in the body? Exactly. Everything.

When you start breathing full big breaths of air, you get the fluid moving, and the brain and spinal cord will work better. And with your brain and spinal cord working better, everything in your body can improve, including the way you think and how smart you are. Your moods, emotions and energy levels could improve as well. Everything.

The last reason why breathing is so important is, in my opinion, the most important. That is the scanning of the body and mind. With each breath, your body does a self-check. Your body checks itself out, and figures out if anything needs to be adjusted. And the full breath corresponds to your entire body/mind complex. If you skip part of the breath cycle, you skip part of the self-check. Breathing in fully scans things like your thoughts and emotions. Breathing out fully, or the bottom of the breath cycle, scans the bones, muscles, and organs. If you skip any part of the breath cycle, you are skipping that part of the self-check. Now let me ask you something: If your body does not know something is wrong and needs to be fixed, what are the odds that it will fix it? Not very good.

Simply breathing in fully will often "wake your body up" to what it needs to do. And it is often just the act of realizing what needs to be done that gets things done. So breathing in and out fully, every day, allows your body to check in every day and figure out what it needs to do.

So how do you breathe? Everyone has a different theory on how that should be. I say, deeply and fully, and leave the rest up to you. Listen to your inner knowing, and do what it says. What I mean by deeply and fully is simply this:

Once each day, take 10 deep breaths of fresh air outside. That means, when you are outside, breathe in all the way, filling up your entire lungs. The top and bottom part. Then, breathe out fully, letting all the air leave your lungs, even squeezing it out a little at the end. And then repeat this nine more times.

Whether you breathe in through your nose and out your mouth or the other way around or whatever, I don't think makes that big a difference. I am not saying it doesn't make a difference. I am saying, I think the biggest point is to make sure you actually breathe these full deep breaths. Once you begin doing that, see what your inner knowing says is right for you. And then do it that way.

Breathing full breaths of fresh air is so important for so many reasons, but the reasons are not important, as long as you breathe 10 full deep breaths every day of fresh air.

1. Communication - Listening, Acting and Requesting
2. Rest – Mental and Physical
3. Breathing- Full Breaths of Fresh Air
4. Food and Water - Quality and Quantity
5. Sunlight
6. Activity - Physical and Mental
7. Consciousness

Food and Water

The diet wars and confusion will now be cleared up, all in one easy sentence. Are you ready? Everyone is different.

The best diet for one person is not going to be the best diet for everyone else. You are different than everyone else. What food is best for you is not necessarily going to be what is right for everyone else. Some people do well on meat, others don't. Some people are fine with lots of carbs, others not. What food is best for you is really dependent on you and your lifestyle.

I will make it really simple to help you figure out what is good. There are a couple of general rules of thumb that apply to everyone. They are really simple. Are you ready?

1. Fresh
2. Pure

Fresh and Pure. It is that simple. All the food you eat, no matter what kind you eat, should be fresh and pure. It is that simple. Then, just listen to your inner knowing, and it will tell you what to eat that is fresh and pure.

If you are craving steak, eat steak. If you want veggies, eat veggies. If you want some fruit, eat fruit. If you want some nuts or seeds, eat nuts and seeds. When your choices of food are always from the fresh and pure categories, you will eat exactly what you need to eat without having to worry about your carbs, calories, fat, cholesterol, or anything. It's so simple.

One of the most common reasons people do not eat healthier food is because it is more expensive. They have a hard time justifying spending more money on better food. I will show you why it is worth it to spend the extra money now.

It is actually more expensive to buy regular food. When you eat regular poisoned and adulterated food, it costs you your health. What that means is that you are not as productive, you have less energy, you get sick more often and have to take more sick days, your moods are erratic, and you don't function as well. How much does this cost you? If your kids have to stay home three extra days every school year because they are sick, how much does that cost you? It actually costs you more to buy the regular food. The extra money you pay for healthy food actually ends up saving you money. It is just elsewhere in your life that the money gets saved.

The biggest and best reason why fresh and pure food is so worth it, is: How much is it worth for you to be happy and feeling great all of the time? How much is it worth for life to be easier on your kids, for them not to be sick as often? How much is your children's happiness worth? Good quality food improves the health of your body, and thereby your moods and emotions. No food tastes as good as your health and *bazuji* feeling.

Much of the rest of this section on food is sharing information about all the myths, limited vision, and false ideas that are out there about food and diets. The key is to remember fresh and pure and what it means.

Fresh

So what does fresh and pure mean? Fresh generally means not in a can or box. Most things that are put into cans and boxes are old and dead. The life force has been long gone from the food. It is no longer fresh. Now, stuff in a box or can can be fresh, but it usually isn't. Frozen stuff can go either way. Frozen stuff is usually fresher than boxed or canned stuff. It has to be, because it cannot last as long frozen as it can in a box or can.

How do you know if the boxed, canned, or frozen food is fresh? Right now, you don't. Unfortunately most food does not come with a "born on" date. It should, but it doesn't. So what do you do? You make sure a good portion of your food comes from places other than a box, a can, or the freezer. If most of your food is coming from fresh sources, you will not have to worry about the little that is not.

There are two big reasons, and hundreds of little reasons, why non-fresh food is bad for you. The biggest is because of the life force value food has. The other is that old food has fewer vitamins and nutrients that are needed by your body to do everything your body does.

What is the life force value of food? It is a number that, I will be the first to admit, has not yet been measured by science and quantified. The life force value of food is another form of energy, like calories. It is used by your body for processes and functions on a day-to-day basis. In the traditional Chinese systems, there is a measurement for this. They call it taste. The taste of the food has an energy, or life force. This energy value is converted by your body for its own energy needs. The longer a food is lying around or processed before you eat it, the less life force energy or taste it has.

You can easily measure this. Have you ever eaten garden-fresh peas or cucumbers or apples or strawberries or raspberries, or anything that you picked and immediately ate? Doesn't it always taste so much better than anything you have every bought in a store? Yes. That difference in taste is the life force value, or the taste of the food, as the traditional Chinese system calls it.

Fresh food has more life force energy than non-fresh food. This is extra energy your body uses to do everything it does. With less energy available, your body has less energy. Most junk food has no life force value, even though it has lots of taste. This "false taste or energy value" leaves you with no extra energy. That is one big reason why, when someone eats only junk food, they have no energy to do much of anything, and why they are always hungry. The life force energy is missing, because the food is not fresh.

The longer food sits around, the fewer vitamins and nutrients the food contains. Many vitamins and nutrients your body needs to function break down with time. They also break down with heating, cooling, freezing, and many other mechanical processes that are done to our food today.

Let me give you a little example of why vitamins and minerals are so important. If you want to build a brick house, what do you need? Well, you need bricks and mortar, and wood, and windows and doors. You need some basic stuff to build that house. What if you don't have bricks, or mortar or windows or doors? How well do you think the house will function after you are done "trying" to build it? Not very well.

Vitamins, minerals and nutrients are like the bricks, mortar, windows, doors, wood, etc. of the house. They are the parts that your body uses to build you. If you don't give your body those key building blocks, things in your body are not going to work very well.

If you try to substitute cheap, not so good imitations, if you tried to build a brick house with a bunch of rocks, the house would not be as good. If you tried to use old, warped windows, the house would not function very well. If you used wood that had holes in it and was not complete, your house would not be very functional.

The same is true of your body. You can get good vitamin and mineral sources, or you can get cheap, not so good, imitation vitamins with parts missing. Which one do you think will be better for you? Of course, the ones that are whole, complete, and have everything your body needs to build itself healthy and strong again.

This means if you are going to take supplements, make sure you get them from a good source. If the supplements are really cheap, well, you usually get what you pay for. One of the best sources I have ever found is a company called Standard Process www.standardprocess.com. The only problem with them is, you cannot buy them yourself. You have to go through some doctor or other medical professional. Their website will help you find one if you want to go this route.

There are other good lines of supplements as well, but none I will name here because, in my opinion, it really is worth going through someone to get the best. Standard Process is the best, in my opinion. But they are kind of like the computer company Macintosh. They refuse to settle and let just anyone use their technology, but rather highly control how it is used. This means that other supplement companies are bigger and more popular, but not as good.

I also have a few more product recommendations on my website.

Pure

This means nothing artificial and nothing added, including poisons, pesticides or, one of the biggest culprits, refined carbohydrates, commonly called sugar. Sugar is added to almost everything in a regular grocery store. Even many things in a supposed "health food store" have sugar added.

The average American eats over 300 pounds of sugars each year. Most of this is because of all the sugar that is added to the everyday foods most people eat. Refined carbohydrates include anything that ends in "ose." Sucrose, fructose, glucose, lactose, maltose, dextrose, corn syrup, high fructose corn syrup and sugar all count as sugar. An easy way to remember this is anything that rhymes with "gross."

I am not talking about sugar naturally found in fruits and other such sources. If nature put it there, it is usually fine. And again, how it affects you will depend more on you individually than the type of fruit itself. Yes, sugar is natural, but it is not fresh. And when you add it to another food, the other food is not pure either.

Refined carbohydrates also come in the form of grains and flours. Most pasta, bread, flour, and other grain-based products are refined, almost to the point of sugar, and to the point where the refined carbohydrates respond in the body the same way sugar does.

There are two big reasons why refined carbs and sugar are so bad, as well as hundreds of smaller reasons. The two big reasons are these:

1. Refined carbs and sugar have no vitamins, minerals, or anything else that is needed to operate and run a healthy body
2. Refined carbs and sugar cause blood sugar levels to be artificially raised and lead to all the problems that come with high blood sugar levels.

First, the refining process takes away all the vitamins and minerals that are naturally found in whatever plant is being refined. There is nothing left but pure carbohydrates. In case you missed it, see above why vitamins and nutrients are so important for your body and life.

The second reason is that refined carbs drastically alter your blood sugar levels. What is the big deal with this? The easiest to show you is what happens to you after you eat. You get really tired and lethargic. You have trouble staying awake and you want to go to sleep. Guess what? The rest of your body is doing the same thing. Your cells are going into a "sugar coma." Your mind, which controls everything, is also going to sleep on the job. Your brain is not doing everything it needs to do to keep you functioning properly. And if your brain is not doing its job properly, anything could be going wrong with your body, and often is.

Refined carbs/sugars are actually the biggest contributing factor to type 2 diabetes—that is, the type of diabetes people develop later in life. The major contributing factor to type 2 diabetes is eating too many refined carbs. Type 2 diabetes is one of the easiest things for your body to heal. Are you ready? It is so simple. Quit eating carbs. It really is that simple. I have yet to meet anyone who was a type 2 diabetic who could not totally control their blood sugar levels without any insulin just by cutting carbs out of their diet.

Refined carbs/sugars also are one of the main contributing factors to high cholesterol levels and heart disease. I also have yet to meet anyone who has cut refined carbs and sugars out of the food that they eat, and did not have their cholesterol levels go down. I have a free Cholesterol Lowering Report for anyone who signs up for my newsletter at my website, as well as a couple of other free bonuses.

Pure also means no other added ingredients. This means organic. If something is not organic, I promise you, it will have poisons on/in it. These poisons are the chemicals that farmers use to kill the bugs and weeds that are really hard to kill. Now let me ask you a question. Have you ever tried to get rid of some bug in your house that is really hard to kill? Do you know how hard it is to get rid of those bugs once you have them, how toxic the stuff is that finally kills the bugs? Well, the same is true of the bugs that farmers have a hard time getting rid of. They often use really poisonous chemicals to kill those bugs. In fact, they are so poisonous that the warning labels on the chemicals they use would scare you. And these substances go directly onto any food crop that is not organic.

Now, the FDA says these pesticides are used in "safe amounts." But I will remind you that the FDA has said many things are "safe" that they now say are highly toxic and cancer causing. DDT is the best example that most people know about. For the longest time, the FDA said DDT was completely safe, and now it is considered one of the worst known poisonous chemicals. My point is to use your common sense here. If something kills those really hard-to-kill bugs, do you really want it inside you, no matter how little of it there is? I don't. just because the FDA says it is safe now does not mean they will not change their minds in the future. They have done this many times before.

There are many natural, completely safe methods of controlling bugs and weeds. Many farmers just don't know about them, because all they are sold are the chemicals from the herbicide and pesticide companies. This is kind of like the drug reps who sell doctors all the drugs they use. These reps sell all the farmers the chemicals they use. There is no fortune to be made in natural methods of controlling bugs and weeds, so there are no reps pushing these natural methods that are just as effective, if not more effective, in controlling bugs and weeds.

Pure includes something being organic.

It is my position that if a food product meets the categories of both fresh and pure, it is not inherently bad, ever. This includes dairy products and animal products as well.

Dairy has a pretty bad rap out there. Considering the way most dairy products show up on the shelf, I agree; the stuff is bad. But most dairy is not fresh or pure when it ends up on the shelves. First, most dairy cows are injected with growth hormones to get them to produce more milk, and this female growth hormone goes straight into the milk. If you want a boost of female growth hormones in your body, then hey, nothing wrong. But this artificial female growth hormone is not good for anyone. It messes up the whole endocrine balance in the body, which includes menstrual cycles, moods, emotions, acne, and many other things.

Then there is the pasteurization process. It kills much of the good bacteria that are found in milk. Pasteurization also destroys most of the nutrients and vitamins that are naturally found in milk. Yes, it gets rid of some of the bacteria that may cause sickness. But I refer you to the earlier chapter, where I stated that the key component in getting sick is not the bacteria. If dairy were found in its natural fresh and pure state, I would not see a problem with it. In fact, most people who cannot tolerate dairy products almost never have a problem with organic raw dairy products. Organic raw dairy is fresh and pure.

Animal products and meat are another controversial topic. Are they good for you or not? My view on the subject is similar to my view on dairy. If the animal products are fresh and pure, they are not inherently bad in any way, shape or form. In fact, if meat and other animal products are healthily and humanely raised, they can be great.

Meat and animal products as they are today, however, are not fresh and pure. They are full of chemicals, growth hormones, toxins, fear, and God knows what else. These types of meat and animal products are not good for you. And these are most of the meat and animal products that are in your traditional supermarket today.

I will give you a small glimpse of what is common in the industry today. Over 90% of all the chickens raised in America today are raised like this: They have a cage big enough to stand up and sit down in. They get no fresh air or sunlight their entire life. They are fed tons of hormones and antibiotics. The leftover chicken parts that cannot be used for anything else are ground up and fed them back to the other chickens. This just further concentrates the hormones and antibiotics in the chickens. They grow up in seven weeks instead of the 12-16 weeks that it would take them naturally.

Most cows are raised in a similar fashion, with hormones and chemicals, under unnatural conditions, and they are slaughtered even more inhumanely. Fear is a chemical reaction in the body, which is why dogs can smell it. The fear of death the cows experience right before they die is "locked" into the meat as they are killed, and then you eat it. Most cattle are starved and given nothing to drink or eat for days before they are slaughtered, so that it is easier to butcher them. This meat is not fresh or pure, either.

This is only a touch of what goes on. I have spared you many of the gory details about what happens with traditional meat before you eat it. There is good news. Animals can be healthily and humanely raised. They can get fresh air and sunlight. They can remain chemical free, and be treated with respect and killed without pain or fear. When this is done, the meat not only tastes better, but it is actually some of the healthiest meat available. In fact, free-range grass-fed organic beef, butchered humanely, is some of the healthiest food available, and is a great source of omega 3 essential fatty acids. Ingesting these essential fatty acids, along with eliminating sugar, is an almost guaranteed way to prevent heart disease. In fact, the ratio of omega 3 to omega 6 essential fatty acids is even better in this type of beef than in fish.

There is one group of people who insist that even this type of meat is not humane because it is still taking a life. To address this, I have a little story. It is about a hunting trip. This trip isn't about any ordinary hunter. It is about a hunter who actually has respect for the animal being killed, and it is amazing how easy it is to go hunting this way. It is as if the animal is "giving themselves to you." They see you and yet they just stand there and offer themselves to you. It is as if they are honored to be able to serve you and be your feast. The aboriginal people in Australia, the Native Americans in America long ago, and many other cultures around the world all report the same thing. That it is a blessing for the animal to give themselves over to be eaten by you. All it requires is respect on the part of the person eating the meat.

If meat is healthily and humanely raised, it can be one of the greatest sources of nutrients. There is no one thing that is inherently bad, as long as it is fresh and pure. Those are words to live by.

Choose foods that you want to eat, that sound good to you, that are fresh and pure. Listen to your inner wisdom and what it is telling you to eat, and you will be just fine. Dieting is really that simple.

Some people are better off not eating late at night, others are. Some people do well skipping breakfast, others don't. Some people do well with three big meals, others do better snacking all day long. Some do better with variety, some do better with the same thing over and over again. It is really different for everyone. And as long as you are choosing from the fresh and pure categories and listening to your inner knowing, you will be eating perfectly for you.

Water

I could write a whole book about water. Wait, someone already did. In fact, there are a couple books. My favorite is *Your Body's Many Cries For Water*, written by F. Batmanghelidj, M.D. He has a couple of other books and, of the ones I have read, that is my favorite. It basically explains everything I am about to say here, butin the length of a book. Check it out if you doubt anything I am saying here.

First, how much water is ideal to drink? According to the US Government, everyone is the same and we all need 6-8 glasses a day. Well, guess what? Everyone is different. We all need different amounts. As a general guideline, we should drink one quart (32 ounces, four cups, or .9 liters) of water for every 50 pounds of bodyweight. A 150-lb person needs three quarts of water a day.

Many people cannot imagine how they can drink that much water, because most people do not think of this option: Quit drinking the other fluids you are drinking. I promise you, if you drink only water, you will easily, probably without any effort, drink that amount of water. If you want to keep drinking all the other fluids you normally drink, yes, it will require more effort and you will have to go to the bathroom more. But if you give up the other fluids, it will save you money, because water is much cheaper than any other drink.

This is for when you first begin drinking water. You need more to catch up, to bring your body back to a place where it does not need as much water. When you actually become hydrated and less toxic, you need less and less water to do everything that needs to be done in your body.

The quality of the water you drink is just as important as quantity. So what counts as water? Water. That is it. The only thing that counts as water to your body is water. If you put lemon, or lime, or tea, or minerals, or electrolytes, or sugar, or colorings and flavorings, or anything else in the water, it does not count as water. Your body does not utilize it the same as it would pure water, and here is why:

These next couple of paragraphs are technical, and are only essential to prove that the only thing that counts as water is water. You do not need to know or memorize this as long as you just drink plain water. Here it is:

There is a process in nature called osmosis. It is when the water moves across a membrane to balance out the osmotic pressure. Simply put, it means that water moves all by itself to the area with the least amount of anything else in it. For example, take a container of water and put a filter or membrane down the middle of the container. This membrane only lets water through, not salt. You then pour salt into only one side of the container and let it set.

After a while, something interesting will happen. You will end up with a water level that is higher on the side containing the salt. Water will actually move up against gravity, and be higher on the side you put the salt into. This is because there was a higher concentration of "stuff," in this case salt, on one side, and the water moved to that side. This movement of water from a low concentration of stuff to a high concentration is called osmosis. It is a natural process that happens automatically. The greater the difference in concentration, the faster and more easily the water moves.

When you drink plain, pure water, the water goes into the inside of your intestines. Your blood is mostly water with stuff dissolved in it on the outside of your intestines. The intestinal wall acts like that membrane. It will let water through, but not the stuff in the blood. So the water you drank, automatically, through osmosis, goes into your bloodstream. The concentration of stuff in the blood is more than the concentration of stuff in the water you drank, so the water moves across the intestinal wall, and you absorb the water.

Now, guess what happens when you put stuff in the water you drink? The concentration of the stuff in the water goes up, and the water doesn't move across the intestinal wall as easily. Now the body has to actively absorb the water. And in the process of doing this, the water is used up, so to actively absorb water takes more water, and your net effect of absorbed water is not very much. So, yes, technically you do get water from sources where the water has stuff in it. But the amount you get is far less than if you drink just plain water.

To give you an idea, if you drink tea or soda, you will need to drink almost four times as much in order to get the same amount of usable water into your blood. I don't know about you, but I don't want to drink four gallons of liquid a day. My recommendation is, stick to good old-fashioned plain, pure water.

Where do you get good water? The best water is pure water in its natural state, which is unfortunately not readily available. Water that has been unexposed to the environment for the last 200 years is about the only source. Nariwa is a water from Japan that is very close to pure. The only drawback is the price—$5 USD for 500 ml. Not cheap. There is a great website and book that will shock you about water and how different water really is: www.ohno.org

A generally great, consistent, much cheaper form of water is Reverse Osmosis (RO) water. You can purchase a good filter for home use, or you can buy the water already filtered at Whole Foods Market or most other grocery stores. The water you fill your own containers with at grocery stores is usually good quality reverse osmosis water. Either way, if you buy a filter, make sure it is a good one. Some units are no better than simple Brita filters.

Now, here is something you can do to get the best of both worlds. You can put 1 oz of Nariwa water into a gallon of RO water. Let it set for a couple minutes, and you now have a gallon of water that is almost the same as the original Nariwa water, for much less.

For the best filters I have found, with the best warranties, go to www.ewater.com. They also carry the Nariwa water I mentioned above. When you get to the site, enter the referral code A2256 and the price code 99p1 and you will receive a 15% discount on most products. They have a six-month unconditional money back guarantee. No matter what, if for any reason you are not completely satisfied within the first six months, you can send whatever you ordered back for a full refund, no questions asked. You cannot beat that. The company offers this because their products are so exceptional that very few people return them. If you want the best, they have it. If you want the cheapest, I warn you, you will get what you pay for.

Pur or Brita type filters would be a cheaper way to go, but the quality of the water is less. Pur is a brand name filter like Brita. These filters take out some of the impurities, but not nearly as many as the reverse osmosis units. One of the other bad things is that they add back in silver nitrate, a heavy metal. The resulting water is better than tap water, but a far cry from optimum.

There is a debate in the health care community about which water is best. People will usually recommend one of two types of water, reverse osmosis or distilled water. RO water is sent through a series of filters, and what you end up with is pure water with nothing in it or added. Distilled water has been boiled, and the steam condensed back into water.

The pros and cons of each: RO machines take the minerals out of the water, minerals your body needs that are naturally found in water. But the question is, how much? How much of these minerals would you actually absorb and use if they were left in the water?

First, the minerals found in water are in ionic form, which just means they are little positive-charged molecules. Your digestive tract is positively charged also. Everyone who has played with magnets knows, like repels like. The same sides of the magnets repel each other. The positively charged ions and your positively charged intestines mean that the minerals are repelled from the lining of your digestive tract. And, to be absorbed, they have to not only come near the lining, but pass across it. This means you will not absorb most of the minerals in water, even if they are there.

The amount of minerals you would actually absorb from non-reverse osmosis water is really small. In comparison to the amount of minerals you absorb on a daily basis, the amount is insignificant. As of now, there is no machine I know of that takes out all the chemicals and leaves in the minerals.

Distilled water takes out some toxins, and leaves in most minerals, but is really bad water to drink, for a couple reasons. It is dead water, and it is toxic water.

First, dead water. Water is more than H_2O. Water is two atoms of hydrogen (H), one of oxygen (O) and energy. This energy is vitally important. Distillation removes a lot of this energy. What you are left with is dead water that the body cannot easily utilize. In Europe and many parts of the world, the idea of drinking distilled water is crazy. The simplest way to show you why is to do an experiment. Water your plants with only distilled water. See what happens to them. See how long they live. The distilled water kills your plants, because the water is dead.

Second, distilled water is toxic. Here is how the distillation process works: The water is boiled; the steam that evaporates is then condensed into distilled water. In the average water supply in America, there are over 250 known chemicals poisonous to humans. On average, about 100 of these chemicals boil at a temperature lower than water. This means the chemicals boil up into steam, and then they are condensed along with the water. The resulting distilled water has all the chemicals that boiled at a temperature lower than water.

So my general recommendation is RO water. Listen to your inner knowing. It may tell you to drink some other type because, bottom line, everyone is different. There are different filters, and different sources of bottled water, different this and that, etc. Listen to your inner knowing and what it tells you to drink. And remember, this might change over time.

You can buy filtration units to make RO water from your tap water at home, or you can fill up your own containers at most grocery stores. You can also buy RO water on the run. Aquafina and Dasani are the products that Pepsi and Coke put out. They are reverse osmosis water. There are others; just read the label. If it is RO water, it will say so.

In fact, as a funny side note, Aquafina and Dasani use the same water they start with to make RO water, then put additives, flavorings, sugar and other products in it to make soda. They sell the water with less time and stuff put into it, usually in the same containers they sell soda in, for twice the price of soda.

Remember, do not buy water with artificial stuff added. If you do, the body does not get as much usable water from the same amount of water. Drink fresh and pure water, just like your food, fresh and pure.

Now that you know where to get good water, why drink water? Here is my favorite, easiest explanation of why. Electricity travels over water. Water is the main way that nerve impulses, which control your entire being, travel over the water in your nerves. Without water to do this, your body cannot control and regulate itself correctly, leaving you with less than optimum *bazuji*, healing capacity and well being. Ok, actually it is not the water, but the stuff in the water that conducts electricity. But without the water, there is no place for the "stuff in the water" to conduct the electricity, so it's same principle.

How do you drink water? Room temperature, cold, gulping sipping? Whatever way you want to drink it. Everyone is different. Listen to your inner knowing and it will tell you how to drink your water. You will have a preference of one way over another, and that is probably your inner knowing telling you what to do.

The website for Dr. B, the guy who wrote the book I mentioned above, is www.watercure.com. Some of the things Dr. B says that drinking water has helped the body heal are: stomach pain, ulcers, hiatal hernia, false appendix pain, rheumatoid arthritis pain, low back and neck pain, angina (heart pain), stress and depression, high and low blood pressure, high cholesterol, overweight, asthma, allergies, diabetes, sleeping problems, anxiety, mood swings, bad eyesight, memory loss, poor clarity of thought, and nervousness, just to name a few. Wouldn't it make sense that if you drink water and the body healed these conditions, then by drinking water it could also prevent some of these from happening, and more?

Some people report that they are not able to drink water, the water going right through them, they don't like the taste of water, or they feel bloated when they drink a lot of water. When you add enough health to your level of *bazuji*, these symptoms, just like any other symptom, will go away. Be someone who is *bazuji*, and do what it takes to add to your level of *bazuji*.

What about the myth that drinking too much water is bad for you? What a joke! My question is, how much is too much? Most of the cases of people dying from drinking too much water I could find involved athletes competing in extreme events, or hazing rituals on campuses. I could not find one case of someone drinking water as you or I would and dying from it. Not one.

Our bodies are 70% water. It should be no surprise to anyone that you need water to function. Everything in your body needs water in some way or another in order to function. So enjoy.

Drink pure water with nothing added. RO is usually best, but listen to your inner knowing. After you are hydrated and *bazuji*, half your bodyweight in ounces is a good amount of water to drink. Adjust to your needs accordingly using your inner knowing.

1. Communication - Listening, Acting and Requesting
2. Rest - Physical and Mental
3. Breathing - Full Breaths of Fresh Air
4. Food and Water - Quantity and Quality
5. Sunlight
6. Activity - Physical and Mental
7. Consciousness

Sunlight

Getting healthy amounts of sunlight on your skin and in your eyes is a very important part of adding to your level of health and *bazuji*. The sun does all kinds of wonderful things for your *bazuji*. The easiest way to show you how much we need the sun is this.

All life on the planet is dependent on the sun. Without the sun, there would be no life on the planet. All life is dependent on the sun. Plants convert the sunlight into energy, and all animals need plant life or other animals in order to live. All life in nature is dependent on the sun. We as humans are part of nature. We need sunlight just like everyone else.

Vitamin D is a vitamin found in only a handful of foods, but it is a vitamin your body produces when your skin is exposed to direct sunlight. Vitamin D is essential for you to be *bazuji*. There is tons of scientific evidence to actually support this as well.

There is also something called S.A.D. or Seasonal Affective Disorder. This just means that, in the winter, some people become sad. This is because of a lack of sunlight. The treatment is having the person sit under artificial lights that put out light very similar to the sun. These lights are called SAD boxes. They are just boxes with special lights to simulate the sunlight.

Sunlight is essential for your life and *bazuji*. This often brings up the concern of skin cancer. People are told the sun causes skin cancer and they should wear sunblock to prevent skin cancer. This is a big fat theory of the medical symptom and disease care profession. Skin cancer is dramatically on the rise because people are supposedly spending more time in the sun, and this is the supposed "proof" that skin cancer is caused by the sun. Did the experts happen to notice that most cancer is on the rise? Does the sun cause these cancers as well?

I ask you this: Show me any proof, any study, anything. Nope, just theories and the fact that the incidence of skin cancer is higher today and the doctors link this to a supposed increase in sun exposure.

There is actually proof that the sun is safe and good for you from a medical doctor at Boston University Medical School, Michael Holick, MD. His book, *The UV Advantage*, shares with you exactly what I am talking about, that the sun is healthy for you.

This is also another perfect example of how non-scientific the medical community is. They came up with their theory that the sun is the cause of skin cancer, and they are fighting tooth and nail to hold onto it. So much so that Dr. Holick was forced to resign from his position because of his contradicting beliefs about sunlight exposure. Science changes with new information. Medicine does not. The medical profession ignores new findings as long as they can, until the evidence becomes so overwhelming that they are forced to change or look like the fools they are.

Well, my friends, I have a question for you. How many other bad things are on the rise that people are doing? Lots. Just because the sun hits the skin, the powers that be say it means that is the one thing that "causes" skin cancer. They are looking for the one cause and one cure. Remember, what is the one cause of anything? Lack of *bazuji*. That is it. If you do not have enough *bazuji*, you will get symptoms, and the factors from your life and the environment will determine what symptoms and/or disease you express.

Remember, what is cancer? It is a mutated cell growing and dividing without the body killing it. There are many things that can contribute to mutated cells, and many things that contribute to your body's not being able to get rid of the cancer cells. You get skin cancer every day, and every day your body kills it.

The sun in and of itself, I say, is not a contributing factor to skin cancer. In my opinion, being burned by the sun is one of the major contributing factors to skin cancer. Most people get no exposure to the sun for months; then they play weekend warrior and go out in the sun all weekend, often getting burned. My inner knowing tells me it is this burning that is a major contributing factor to skin cancer, not the actual sun exposure.

So if you do not build up to being in the sunlight, and you know you will be in the sun for a long time, use a chemical-free sunblock.

The irony about sunblock is the stuff most people use actually contains a chemical that is known and admitted to cause cancer. The FDA says PABA is a known carcinogen, and yet it is in most sunblocks. This is ironic. Now, there are PABA-free sunscreens. My thought is that those chemicals that replace the PABA will soon be identified as carcinogens as well. Just give them time. PABA was labeled "safe" by the FDA at first.

My recommendation: get a good chemical-free sunblock. Many health food stores will have them. If you cannot find some elsewhere, there are some featured on my website. Unfortunately, they are not available everywhere right now.

Earlier I said sunlight on your skin and in your eyes. I DO NOT mean look directly at the sun. What I mean is to be outside, without sunglasses, glasses or contacts between you and the sun. Being outside when it is daylight means sunlight is going into your eyes and hitting a part of your eye called the retina. It is the back part of your eye. Well, hitting this back part of your eye stimulates all kinds of processes in the body for bazuji to be present in your body. Glass and plastic filter out parts of the sun's rays. And if you have sunglasses, glasses, or contacts on, you are reducing beneficial parts of the sunlight that are getting into your eyes. You are reducing the healthy benefits of the sunlight.

The myth of the sun causing cataracts also needs to be addressed here. The sun does not cause them. There is no one cause. The sun is not even a major contributing factor to cataracts. Just like every other disease, the only real cause is a lack of health, along with everything that contributed to your lack of health.

The easiest way to get sunlight is go outside. Go outside every day without contacts or any type of glasses and large amounts of your skin exposed to the sun. For you this might not be feasible, because you live some place where there is a thing called winter. So an acceptable alternative is getting some full spectrum light bulbs for your work and home. These are just light bulbs that put out light similar to the sun. You can order them online or at my website. But be careful; not all full spectrum bulbs are created equal. Most of the full spectrum bulbs in traditional stores are not much of an improvement over ordinary lights.

A fun alternative is going south for the winter. Go someplace where you can hang out in the sun without glasses or contacts, with much of your skin exposed to the sun.

Either way, you need sunlight all year round to be *bazuji*.

1. Communication - Listening, Acting and Requesting
2. Rest - Physical and Mental
3. Breathing - Full Breaths of Fresh Air
4. Food and Water - Quantity and Quality
5. Sunlight
6. Activity - Physical and Mental
7. Consciousness

Activity

Activity means both mental and physical activity. To start off, what is the best form of physical activity?

If you have been paying attention, you might be a little hesitant to answer because you know everyone is different. How can there be any one form of physical activity that is best for everyone? You would be right. However, the best form of physical activity is what you will actually do often. That is it. What you will actually do. And the good news is, it can be something different every day. You can walk one day, run another, go swimming another, play Frisbee golf another, go golfing the next, rollerblade the next day, ride your bike another day, etc. You do not have to do the same thing every day. But you can if you want to.

Some hints on listening to your inner knowing around physical activity: One day 30 minutes might be perfect for you, and the next day only 10 minutes is good. Other days an hour or two might be ideal. One day a slow relaxing pace might be ideal, the next a heavy vigorous workout might be called for. There are no rules about how and when you should or shouldn't do physical activity. My only guideline would be: Do what you want to do, and listen to your inner knowing when doing it. The lawyers would want me to tell you to consult a physician before starting any exercise program here. My thought is, your inner knowing knows better than any doctor does about what is best for you. If you listen to your inner knowing and act on what it says, who cares about the doctor?

Listen to your inner knowing about how long and how intensely to work out. Don't be so concerned with getting 30 minutes in at X heart rate three times a week. Don't be concerned with lifting X pounds X times. Focus more on where you are at right now when you are doing physical activity, and do what is best for you right now.

Walking outside is great. You can take deep full breaths of fresh air when you are walking, go within and focus on the God Presence within you. You will also get sunlight from being outside. You can do four of the seven things in one activity. Walking. How easy is that? In fact, doing any physical activity outside can get you four of the seven things.

Bottom line, just do some form of sustained physical activity.

Mental activity is the same thing. And I am not talking about worry. That is not a constructive mental activity. Wouldn't it be nice if it was? Well, it isn't. When I talk about mental activity, I am talking about creativity, using the mind creatively. It does not have to be "art," either. Creativity comes in many shapes and forms.

You can be a lawyer and be solving cases, figuring out creative ways to win the case. You can be an architect and use your mind to create projects. You can read books and use your mind to create pictures and connections and the "movie in your head." You can do problem solving activities, like crossword puzzles or some card and board games, anything where you are creating new thoughts, new patterns of thinking, and different ways of looking at things. This is mental activity.

Art is also a really good way to have mental activity. The process of creating abstract things also encourages new ways of thinking and patterns of thought. These new ways of thinking and being are stimulating your brain and nerves to grow and regenerate. Like the muscles in the body, if you don't use them, you lose them. So creatively using the mind helps us to grow and flourish from within.

What is the best form of mental activity? Whatever it is you will actually do. And it can be different every day. Just as with physical activity, whatever you do is perfect. It can be the same thing every day, or you can do something different every day. It is really up to you and your inner knowing.

The key is doing mental activity, creating with your mind new things, thoughts, and ways of thinking, whether it is art or how to win a legal case.

1. Communication - Listening, Acting and Requesting
2. Rest - Physical and Mental
3. Breathing - Full Breaths of Fresh Air
4. Food and Water - Quantity and Quality
5. Sunlight
6. Activity - Physical and Mental
7. Consciousness

Consciousness

Consciousness completes not only the list, but the circle. Being conscious ties back into the first thing, communication, and all the others.

Being conscious as you are listening to your inner knowing. Being conscious when you act and do what your inner knowing says. Being conscious with all of your thoughts, words, actions, and feelings so that you ask for only exactly what you want from the Creator. Being conscious so you don't inadvertently ask for something you don't want.

Being conscious as you are actually resting.

Being conscious when you are taking the full deep breaths of fresh air into your body.

Being conscious as you eat your food. Being conscious as you drink your water. Tasting the food and water. Smelling the food and water. Chewing your food consciously. Being aware as you are putting stuff in your body.

Being conscious as you are in the sun, being conscious of anything like glasses or contacts, or windows getting between you and the sun and removing them.

Being conscious as you are doing activity, not zoning out and listening to music or watching TV, almost unconscious and unaware you are even doing activity, but being conscious and having fun as you are creating.

Most importantly, there is being conscious of the God Presence within you, being conscious of the Creator and thy being, the animating force in everything and every one. Being conscious of the connection between you and everyone else. Being conscious that the same God Presence is in all of us.

We are all connected as one. All humans are of the same essence. Religion seems to get in the way, but there is a way that I have heard which explains religion and God beautifully in my mind.

Imagine a bunch of blind people all standing around an elephant. One has the ear, another has the nose, another has the tail, another has the foot, another has the body, another has the head, etc. Someone comes along and asks the people what they have. And they all describe something different. They then begin arguing and fighting over who is right. They all are. They all have true parts of the whole. It is just that the parts seem to be different and contradicting. And when considering the whole they are all right.

I view religion as the same thing. It is all true, because we as humans are mostly, essentially blind when it comes to the true and full nature of GOD. Everyone is a part of the whole, and they are all true. Even though as the parts they seem contradicting, they are all different parts of the same whole.

Understanding and being conscious of the interconnectedness among us all. We are all one. You are they, and they are you. When you see and are conscious of this connection all humans have, it creates peace and serenity within you. This peace and serenity is the basis for *bazuji* being present in your body.

You are being conscious of your life.

In summary, here is all it takes to be *bazuji*.

Here are your Action Steps:

1. Communication – Listening, Acting and Requesting
2. Rest – Physical and Mental
3. Breathing – Full Breaths of Fresh Air
4. Food and Water – Quantity and Quality
5. Sunlight
6. Activity – Physical and Mental
7. Consciousness – Being conscious

And here is the really great news about all of this: All of these seven things tie into each other. They do not add to each other in a linear way. $1 + 1$ does not equal 2. With these things, $1 + 1 = 4$. And $1 + 1 + 1 = 9$.

When you do two of these things, they build on each other in an exponential way. When you do three or four of these things, they work even better.

Let me give you an example: When you drink water, it makes the various processes in your body work better. You have the water needed to exchange the oxygen better when you breathe. You have the water needed to better absorb the nutrients from the food you eat. You have the energy to do more physical activity. Your body can communicate better with all its different parts. Everything works better.

And when you take deep full breaths of fresh air, you have more oxygen to absorb the water better. You have more oxygen for exercising so you are not as tired, you have more oxygen to absorb the food and nutrients you need better, you have more oxygen for everything your body needs to do.

And it just keeps going. These things multiply each other, not add. The more you do, the greater and greater improvement you see in your life and body.

Adding to your health is what makes you well. Diagnosing and treating only temporarily put a band-aid on the problem. They do nothing to increase your health and help make you well. In fact, they usually reduce your level of health and well being. Whether or not you treat your symptoms and disease, you must keep adding to your health. Whether or not you take herbs and vitamins to combat illness, you must keep increasing your well being. Whether or not you go to the medical symptoms and disease care system, you must keep adding to your health. When you add to your health, your body is able to heal itself the way it was designed to. Keep adding to your health, no matter what else you do, and it will do nothing but help.

When you do all seven of these to their full potential, you will be *bazuji*. You do not have to take my word for it either. You can prove it to yourself. Do these seven things and you will notice positive changes in all areas of your life. You will see the full scope of bazuji manifesting in your life. You will be *bazuji*.

Enjoy it.

Chapter 21

Taking Action:
The Next Step

Now that we have shifted who you are being, these are the actual action steps to take. They help keep your new perspective on *bazuji* in place and actually give you *bazuji*.

Here is where most people get stuck—what to do next, not only with their *bazuji*, but with their life. I will give you a little secret about how to continually leap forward in life, and that is, determining your next step. What is the very next action for you to do?

Most of my examples will be around producing *bazuji* in your life. You can apply this principle of finding the very next thing to do, or action step, to everything in your life.

Action Steps: Contributing Factors

Remember that there is not one cause and one cure. There are many things that contribute to any given sickness and, ultimately, it is a lack of health. As with light and darkness, you must turn on and add to your level of health to make a permanent difference in your *bazuji*. Don't worry about what the diagnosis is. The question is, how are you going to add to your level of health in your body?

The medical symptoms and disease care system and its doctors do not have answers for you. They do not add to your level of health. The only thing they do is treat symptoms and disease. If your inner knowing ever tells you to go to them, use extreme caution and your own thought and logic when going to the medical symptoms and disease care establishment. Be very aware of your inner knowing and what it is telling you the entire time you are seeking help from the symptoms and disease care people. They may be able to temporarily help you out of a symptom or disease but, overall, they do nothing to increase your *bazuji*.

Cost and Benefit

Whenever you are stuck or getting stuck about doing what your inner knowing is telling you to do, here are some very useful questions to ask yourself. They will help you discover the hidden cost you are paying and find ways around having to give up the immediate benefit you are seeing.

What would I get if I let this go/did this?

What would I lose if I let this go/did this?

What would I get if I didn't let this go/didn't do this?

What would I lose if I didn't let this go/didn't do this?

What benefit do I get? After I don't do what I do, how many and what other ways can I still get this benefit?

Answer these questions out loud around some problem or concern, and the answer to the problem will often be right there. They key is in answering them out loud, even if only to yourself. Watch the problem or concern often disappear.

Symptoms and Disease

Symptoms are your body communicating with you. Your inner wisdom is trying to tell you what it needs to make you be well. If you listen to your inner knowing before you get symptoms, there will be no need for the symptoms. Disease is a label put on a specific group of symptoms, no matter what the contributing factors were for those symptoms. That is why there will never be one cause/one cure for any disease.

Medical Symptoms and Disease Care

It is time to remove the protective veil from a system that is responsible for two million American deaths every year. Remove the laws that make medicine and surgery the reasonable and customary. Give people the freedom to choose for themselves how they want their health care. In the information age, people have tremendous access to information and can easily make informed choices themselves.

It is my belief that when you add to your health, you will not get symptoms or disease. And if you don't have symptoms or disease, there will be no need to go to the medical symptoms and disease care specialists. But if you ever do get symptoms or a disease, listen to your inner knowing first. If it says go, then go. And while you are there, listen to your inner knowing.

If you go to your doctor, and he or she wants to remove some part of your body, ask what would happen if you waited to have the surgery? Many times you can wait a week, a month, or even several months with no adverse effects. If this is your case, start doing the seven things that add to your health, that add to your vitality, to your life, and you will probably be pleasantly surprised when you go back to the doctor and the surgery is no longer needed. But be careful, because many doctors will still want to do the surgery anyway.

If you went to another doctor, and did not tell the new doctor what the other doctor's findings were, and told the new doctor everything else that has happened, what the symptoms were if you had any, and that they are now gone, the new doctor would probably not suggest surgery. The new doctor would probably just monitor the situation. Use your inner knowing. Your inner knowing knows more about your body than all the doctors combined.

If someone is unwilling to be *bazuji* and do what it takes to be *bazuji*, unwilling to be responsible for their own well being, then medical symptoms and disease care can be part of their answer. Anyone who is willing to be in charge of their own *bazuji* will no longer have symptoms and disease, and there will be no need for the medical symptoms and disease care system.

Diagnosis and Treatment

Diagnoses are made up and you cannot treat something that is made up. Diagnosis is a label created from a specific group of symptoms. As there are many contributing factors to those symptoms, there is no way to treat all people with the same diagnosis in the same way. Diagnosis and treatment of a disease don't work.

Belief Systems

Choose belief systems that serve you, belief systems that promote health and well being. This is the second biggest, most important point of my book. Your belief systems are crucial in shaping the world around you.

Be conscious of any negative thoughts you have. They are usually based in negative beliefs. Then change them. Remember that your belief systems, consciously and unconsciously, affect your health and life.

If you have negative belief systems, you are in a state of protection. You are not healing and growing. If you have positive belief systems, you are growing, healing and learning. Changing your belief systems is as simple as choosing to believe something new. If you have a belief system that is not easy for you to change, order my *Change Your Driving Forces* CD set. These CDs will help you easily shift your belief systems.

Inner Knowing

Continue adding to your level of *bazuji* and listening to your inner knowing. If you do, there will be no symptoms or disease to treat, no risk of becoming a medical statistic. You will flow through life with harmony and calmness.

Ask your inner knowing about what to do, what choices and decisions to make, and what is best for you and your family. Ask your inner knowing which health care practitioner to go to, if any. Ask your inner knowing about which way to breathe is best for you. Ask your inner knowing when to rest and how long to rest. Ask your inner knowing what food is best for you and your family. Ask your inner knowing what food you should order at a restaurant and what food to eat at holiday gatherings. Ask your inner knowing how much water you should drink and what kind of water you should drink. Ask your inner knowing how much sunlight you should get. Ask your inner knowing what type of physical and mental activity you should do and how long to do it. Ask your inner knowing to help you remain conscious. Ask your inner knowing about these things often because as you go through life they will often change.

You can also ask your inner knowing about which books to read, which place to go on vacation, which movie to watch, which social event or activity to do, which place to get your hair cut, which place to go to worship, and just about everything else you can imagine. You can ask your inner wisdom for any choice or decision you have to make.

This is how you will always know what is best for yourself and your family with 100% certainty, no matter what comes your way: by asking your inner knowing, listening to your inner knowing and taking action on what your inner knowing says.

Get Your Target

If you have not created your target of health, do that now. Take a couple of moments and figure out what your target looks like. Maybe it looks just like *bazuji*. If not, think about when you are healthy. What would it be like, feel like, what would you be seeing and hearing? What would be happening when you are at your target of health? Imagine the outcome perfectly. Ask for exactly what you want. Focus on that. As you focus on your target, be aware of the things that you know are keeping you from your target.

The more you ask for this, the more you hold your attention and focus on this, the more clearly and exactly you ask, the more quickly your target will show up in your world. You will take action steps and move towards that target naturally. So create your target. Remember, you can change it later if you want. For now, just find one. It will be right and perfect for you. Create your target.

Communication

Begin checking in with your inner knowing. When you are about to make a decision or choice, pause for a moment and listen to what your inner knowing says. Based on all the information and input you have gathered, what does your inner knowing say is the choice to make?

Then take action immediately on what your inner knowing says. Don't question it or second guess it. Go and take the action on your inner knowing's voice.

Often this inner knowing will speak up when you are not expecting it. Your inner knowing will pop up on your radar screen without your even asking. You will be about to do something you have already planned, or something you thought you already made a choice about. Then the inner knowing says "Hey," and tells you to do something differently, or at a different time, or in a different way. Whatever the inner knowing says to you, listen. Be open to the communication and take action immediately.

This inner knowing will never guide you astray or create regrets if you listen to it. When you take action on what your inner knowing is saying to you, you will always be thankful in the end.

Rest

Get both physical and mental rest. Clear your mind before you go to sleep, and your sleep will become very restful. There are other things you can do to get rest as well. Whatever you do, do something. Listen to your inner knowing when it tells you to take a break. You are more productive overall if you take breaks and rest. You produce more even though you work less. When you find yourself very crunched for time, that is the most important time to rest. You will find you have more time.

Breathing

Taking big full breaths of fresh air. Fresh air is outside, possibly inside if you get a good air filter. Simply taking 10 full breaths outside every day is a huge addition to your level of *bazuji*. If you are not going to do this outside, you need to go to my website and purchase the air filter.

Food

I will give you different levels of participation in improving the food you eat. There are two things I want to address first.

One of them is the illusion of limited selection. The funny part is that it is only an illusion. When you go grocery shopping, do you tend to buy the same thing over and over again? Or do you actually take advantage of the selection and buy something different every time? If you are like most people, you probably buy the same thing. Even though there are more choices, you still buy the same thing. With health food choices, you technically have less choice. But once you find something you like, you buy the same thing over and over; the decreased selection really makes no difference.

The second thing is comparing. Do not get caught up in trying to find something that tastes like your old favorite thing. The natural healthy food will not taste the same. It will taste better, if you let it. Let me explain what I mean with a story.

My friend was eating an apple, and after a bite or two, she put the apple down and was going to throw it away. It was one of the worst apples she had ever eaten, she said. Don't ask me why, but I wanted to taste the worst apple ever. I took a bite, and it tasted pretty good to me. And then I had a thought. If I ate the apple expecting an apple taste, it was pretty bad. In fact, horrible. But when I tasted the apple for the taste it had, without comparing it to anything else, it was fine. In fact, the apple was pretty good. My friend, who just a moment ago was going to throw the apple out, tasted it again. When she didn't compare it to what she thought an apple should taste like, she thought it was pretty good as well.

What is the point of this story? If you try to compare the new food you are eating to things you've eaten in the past, it will not be the same. It is not the same. But if you actually taste the new food you are eating for the food it is, you will find it is just as good, if not better, than the food you used to eat. Fresh and pure food always tastes better than toxic food, if you taste the food for what it is.

OK, on to the different levels of eating.

The ultimate choice would be moving to a virgin plot of land in a warm-all-year-round climate, preferably above 6,000 ft in altitude, grow all your own food organically, and raise all the animals you eat yourself. I am not sure this is actually the ultimate, but it makes the other choices seem easier.

No matter which one of the following you choose, listen to your inner knowing the whole time. Listen as you eat. Listen as you buy stuff. Listen and act on what your inner knowing is telling you about the food.

The next best choice is shopping around the outside aisles of a health food store buying only fresh and pure items. The outside aisles of a grocery store are traditionally produce, dairy, meat, and fish. This avoids all the boxes and canned stuff in the middle.

The next level is shopping at a health food store for fresh and pure. Even the stuff in cans and boxes is relatively fresh. Make sure it is pure, which means organic with no sugar or anything else added.

This next one is probably the most benefit you can get with the least amount of effort. Just buy everything at a health food store. Don't worry about what it is, or if it is fresh or pure. Just buy everything you eat at a health food store. This is probably the biggest benefit with the least amount of effort you can get.

The level below that is getting only the health food stuff at your regular grocery store. Most grocery stores in America now have a good selection of health food. Some put it in the aisles by the regular food. Others group it all together. Just buying these products at your regular grocery store is a huge benefit.

The last level is getting as fresh and pure as possible from your regular grocery store. This involves reading labels and getting another book, *Diet for a Poisoned Planet* by David Steinman. It is a book that describes which foods are better for you, all from the non-organic world. Some foods have a tendency to have more chemicals, poisons and pesticides. Others have less. In his book, Steinman gives lists of which non-organic foods are generally safer than others. With this list and by reading labels you can eat healthier even with regular grocery store food.

You need to make sure any form of sugar is not more than number 4 in the ingredients list. Don't read that "new label" that lists the sugars and fats and stuff in a table format. That really tells you nothing. You are interested in the actual list of ingredients in small print on the packaging somewhere. This list is arranged in the order of the highest to lowest percentage of things in the food you are buying.

If any of the sugars is the first ingredient, it is the highest percentage of all the ingredients in that item. Whatever is listed second is the second highest percentage ingredient in that thing, and on down the list. What you are looking for is products where all sugars are lower than fourth on the list. Remember, sugar comes in the form of anything ending in "ose," as well as corn syrup.

You will be amazed when you start reading the labels on everything you purchase, and then you will very quickly realize why the average American eats over 300 pounds of sugars each year. It is in everything you eat, and in large quantities.

If you are following your inner knowing and you want a little extra help finding food that is right for you, there is some help. There is a program called metabolic typing. The book is *The Metabolic Typing Diet* by William Wolcott with Trish Fahey. You answer a bunch of questions, and you then get personalized recommendations for yourself and your unique body based on these questions. They do not give blanket recommendations that are the same for everyone. Metabolic Typing offers the best nutritional recommendations for individuals on a mass market scale. These are better then everything else I have found. My website has information about metabolic typing and how to receive consultations with a professional trained in metabolic typing.

Water

Fresh and pure water as well. The only thing that counts as water is water, and you need about half your body weight in ounces of water each day. Listen to your inner wisdom and what it is saying to you. Remember, thirst is a signal that you are extremely dehydrated. It is a last resort scream from your body for water, just like hunger pangs. These are only present when someone is really, really in need of food. You might have to measure out the amount of water each day and make sure you drink it. You might have to only drink water to make sure you drink all the water your body needs. Whatever you need to do, do it. And start doing it now.

Reverse osmosis water is generally best. This might mean you need to buy an RO machine. This might mean you begin buying water at the grocery store by filling up your own bottles. Or, if you want, you can buy bottled RO water. That tends to get a little pricey, though.

Sunlight

Make plans to go outside every day without contacts or glasses on. Make sure you have lots of skin exposed, getting the direct light of the sun. If you cannot do this all year round where you live, you must get full spectrum lights. You can put them in the regular sockets already in your house where you spend the most time with the lights on. There light bulbs at my website www.Bazuji.com that I recommend.

Activity

This means both physical and mental activity. Do whatever it is you will do, maybe even changing what you do. From running, walking, swimming, rollerblading, biking, lifting weights, aerobics, yoga, dancing—do whatever it is you know you will do. Be creative with your mind. Do anything from art to crosswords to problem solving. Keep stimulating the mind and inventing and creating new ways of thinking and having new thoughts. Figure out what activities you like to do, then set aside time to do these things. Listen to your inner knowing when doing these things. Sometimes you will do them more intensely, sometimes less. The inner knowing will tell you all those details. Listen and act on what it says. Don't get caught up in what your mind says you should do. Remember that your mind, just like everyone else's, knows less than 1% of everything there is to know about your body.

Consciousness

Practice being aware of the inner knowing. Listening to what it says. Act on what your inner knowing says. Remind yourself as often as possible of the interconnectedness of everyone, how we are all of the same nature, the same Creator.

Look for Change

You are searching for more than just how you feel. If you focus on how you feel, you will miss a lot of what is happening. You are looking for what changes are taking place in your life, because the quality of your life is directly dependent on the health of your body. Changes might be any or all of the following and more:

- Sleeping better and more soundly
- Having more energy to do the things you want

- Enjoying improved relationships with people in your life
- Being happier
- Feeling better
- Being more motivated
- Having more time in the day (or so it seems)
- Feeling calm and relaxed
- Being more in touch with yourself/Creator

Really, the changes are limitless. When you are being someone who is healthy and applying what you now know, the results become almost limitless. You will notice these changes if you are looking for changes, so look for changes in your life.

Enjoy and have fun with the great positive changes that will happen!

Go to www.Bazuji.com

Sign up for my free email newsletter to help keep you on track with who you are being. When you sign up for my free newsletter, you will get a bunch of great stuff for free. You will also be automatically entered into a drawing for up to $400 worth of products from Bazuji.com. You will also be notified when my future books are available. The newsletter will also keep you on the cutting edge with additions, improvements, and easier ways that I find to be *bazuji*.

I recommended some products and services in my book and have additional products on my website. Very few people will need all of them. Listen to anything your inner knowing wants you to get or do for you to be well. Realize that it might want something now, and in six months it might want something new.

Taking Action to Do All of These

If you ever get stuck, just think of what your immediate next action is. What is the very next thing you would do if you were going to do something? You will often find that just thinking of this motivates you to go do it. We often get stuck in overwhelm mode, because change seems too daunting, too much to do. But when you just figure out the next step and do it, and the next step, and do it, you get where you want to go. The journey of a thousand miles begins with a single step, and another step, and another. Focus on the next step. The next step is always easy. So take action.

Remember to play. Play the way a child would play. You may not get it right the first time, and then keep at it, playing and having fun with it till you do. Kids keep trying until they learn; that is how they learn. Don't be an adult and give up after the first time it doesn't work. Play like a child, learn, and have fun at the same time.

What's Next

First, if someone told you about this book, or gave you this book, I want you to get in touch with them right now and thank them for that. Let them know how much you liked this book, and thank them for sharing it with you.

Really, do this. Call them, email them, do this right now. Let them know how much you liked this book and how much of a difference it made for you.

Then, tell your friends and family. Get copies for your friends and family and give them this book. If you liked it, so will they.

There are future books already in the works. Not all my books will be for everyone. I know I love authors who tell the truth about what their books are about and who should read them, so you don't have to waste your time. That is what I will do. You now have your inner wisdom to guide you in what to do as well.

The Creators Manual for Your Mind: If you liked *The Creators Manual for Your Body*, this book is a definite recommendation. The message is similar, with an understanding and freedom around the mind, using the full creative power of the mind and harnessing the infinite creative powers of the universe.

When all is said and done, I could sum this book up in a four words: Follow Your Inner Knowing.

Listen to your inner knowing, the inner wisdom inside yourself, your heart brain.

Do what your inner knowing says. Act at once. Act on what it says, act on what it tells you to do, and don't do what it tells you not to do.

Remember that everything you think, do, say, feel, and visualize is a request. Ask for only and exactly what you want, and you will receive the Creator's blessing. The Creator wants to give you everything, if only you are willing to receive.

Follow Your Inner Knowing.

References - Chapter 8
Journal of the American Medical Association, July 26, 2000; 284(4):483-5

Author Affiliation: Department of Health Policy and Management, Johns Hopkins School of Hygiene and Public Health, Baltimore, Md. Corresponding Author and Reprints: Barbara Starfield, MD, MPH, Department of Health Policy and Management, Johns Hopkins School of Hygiene and Public Health, 624 N Broadway, Room 452, Baltimore, MD 21205-1996 (e-mail: bstarfie@jhsph.edu).

References
1. Schuster M, McGlynn E, Brook R. How good is the quality of health care in the United States? *Milbank Q.*1998;76:517-563.
2. Kohn L, Corrigan J, Donaldson M, Eds. *To Err Is Human: Building a Safer Health System.* Washington, DC: National Academy Press, 1999.
3. Starfield *B. Primary Care: Balancing Health Needs, Services, and Technology.* New York: Oxford University Press, 1998.
4. World Health Report 2000. Available at: http://www.who.int/whr/2000/en/report.htm Accessed June 28, 2000.
5. Kunst A. *Cross-national Comparisons of Socioeconomic Differences in Mortality.* Rotterdam: Erasmus University [Press?], 1997.
6. Law M, Wald N. Why heart disease mortality is low in France: the time lag explanation. *BMJ.*1999;313:1471-1480.
7. Starfield B. Evaluating the State Children's Health Insurance Program: critical considerations. *Annul Rev Public Health.*2000;21:569-585.
8. Leape L. Unnecessary surgery. *Annul Rev Public Health.*1992;13:363-383.
9. Phillips D, Christenfeld N, Glynn L. Increase in US medication-error deaths between 1983 and 1993. *Lancet.*1998;351:643-644.
10.Lazarou J, Pomeranz B, Corey P. Incidence of adverse drug reactions in hospitalized patients. *JAMA.*1998;279:1200-1205.
11.Weingart SN, Wilson RM, Gibberd RW, Harrison B. Epidemiology and medical error. *BMJ.*2000;320:774-777.
12.Wilkinson R. *Unhealthy Societies: The Afflictions of Inequality.* London: Routledge; 1996.

13.Evans R, Roos N. What is right about the Canadian health system? *Milbank Q.*1999;77:393-399.

14.Guyer B, Hoyert D, Martin J, Ventura S, MacDorman M, Strobino D. Annual summary of vital statistics 1998. *Pediatrics.*1999;104:1229-1246.

15.Harrold LR, Field TS, Gurwitz JH. Knowledge, patterns of care, and outcomes of care for generalists and specialists. *J Gen Intern Med.*1999;14:499-511.

16.Donahoe MT. Comparing generalist and specialty care: discrepancies, deficiencies, and excesses. *Arch Intern Med.*1998;158:1596-1607.

17.Anderson G, Poullier J-P. *Health Spending, Access, and Outcomes: Trends in Industrialized Countries.* New York: The Commonwealth Fund; 1999.

18.Mold J, Stein H. The cascade effect in the clinical care of patients. *N Engl J Med.* 1986;314:512-514.

19.Shi L, Starfield B. Income inequality, primary care, and health indicators. *J Fam Pract.*1999;48:275-284.

20. *The New England Journal of Medicine.* January 7,1999;340:48,70-76.

References - Chapter 10

1.Lazarou J, Pomeranz BH, Corey PN. Incidence of adverse drug reactions in hospitalized patients: a meta-analysis of prospective studies. *JAMA.* 1998Apr15; 279(15):1200-5.

2.For calculations detail, see "Unnecessary Surgery." Sources: HCUPnet, Healthcare Cost and Utilization Project. Agency for Healthcare Research and Quality, Rockville, MD. Available at: http://www.ahrq.gov/data/hcup/ hcupnet.htm Accessed December 18, 2003. US Congressional House Subcommittee Oversight Investigation. *Cost and Quality of Health Care: Unnecessary Surgery.* Washington, DC: Government Printing Office; 1976. Cited in: McClelland GB, Foundation for Chiropractic Education and Research. Testimony to the Department of Veterans Affairs' Chiropractic Advisory Committee. March 25, 2003.

3.Thomas, EJ, Studdert DM, Burstin HR *et al.* Incidence and types of adverse events and negligent care in Utah and Colorado. *Med Care.* 2000 Mar;38(3):261-71.

Thomas, EJ, Studdert DM, Newhouse JP *et al*. Costs of medical injuries in Utah and Colorado. *Inquiry.* 1999Fall;36(3):255-64. [Two references.]

4.Xakellis GC, Frantz R, Lewis A. Cost of pressure ulcer prevention in long-term care. *Am Geriatric Soc.* 1995May;43(5:496-501.

5.Barczak CA, Barnett RI, Childs EJ, Bosley LM. Fourth national pressure ulcer prevalence survey. *Adv Wound Care.* 1997Jul-Aug;10(4):18-26.

6.Weinstein RA. Nosocomial Infection Update. *Emerg Infect Dis.* 1998Jul-Sep;4(3):416-20.

7.Fourth Decennial International Conference on Nosocomial and Healthcare-Associated Infections. *Morbidity and Mortality Weekly Report.* February 25,2000,Vol.49,No.7:138.

8.Burger SG, Kayser-Jones J, Bell JP. Malnutrition and dehydration in nursing homes: key issues in prevention and treatment. National Citizens' Coalition for Nursing Home Reform. June 2000. Available at: http://www.cmwf.org/programs/elders/burger_mal_386.asp Accessed December 13, 2003.

9.Starfield B. Is US health really the best in the world? *JAMA.* 2000Jul 26;284(4):483-5.

Starfield B. Deficiencies in US medical care. *JAMA.* 2000Nov1;284(17):2184-5.

10.HCUPnet, Healthcare Cost and Utilization Project. Agency for Healthcare Research and Quality, Rockville, MD. Available at: http://www.ahrq.gov/data/hcup/hcupnet.htm Accessed December 18, 2003.

11.Nationwide poll on patient safety: 100 million Americans see medical mistakes directly touching them [press release]. McLean, VA: National Patient Safety Foundation; October 9, 1997.

12.Drug giant accused of false claims. MSNBC News. July 11, 2003. Available at: http://msnbc.com/news/937302.asp?0sl=-42&cp1=1 Accessed December 17, 2003.

13.Tunis SR, Gelband H. Health care technology in the United States. *Health Policy.* 1994 Oct-Dec;30(1-3):335-96.

14.Injuryboard.com. General Accounting Office study sheds light on nursing home abuse. July 17, 2003. Available at: http://

www.injuryboard.com/view.cfm/Article=3005 Accessed December 17, 2003.

15. Rabin R. Caution about overuse of antibiotics. *Newsday.* September 18, 2003.

Centers for Disease Control and Prevention. CDC antimicrobial resistance and antibiotic resistance—general information. Available at: http://www.cdc.gov/drugresistance/community Accessed December 13, 2003.

Everyone you know with a body should read this book. Get them books as presents. Give books as gifts to everyone you care about and love—those who want to be healthy, those you want to be healthy, those who are trying to heal some symptom or disease, people you know with symptoms and disease, people you know without symptoms and disease. This book is for anyone who has a body.

☐ **I am ordering copies of this book for my family and friends $14.95 ea.**
      _____ copies x $14.95 = $_____ (shipping minimal)
Volume discounts available. Call for details.

I am ordering the folwoing CD sets:
☐ **Get Rid of Your Emotional Sh*t and Be Happy**
☐ **Change Your Driving Forces and Naturally Get What You Want**
☐ **Get Rid Of Your Faulty Programming and Beliefs**
☐ **Be Decisive, Making Better Choices, Knowing They Are Right**

One CD set = $179
Second CD set = $129 (total = $308)
Third CD set = $79   (total = $389)
Fourth CD set = $59   (total = $446)
You can get all 4 CD sets for $446. Save $270
(shipping is free if you order 4 sets)
You can also make 4 monthly payments of $120 with a major credit card.
      Total for CD sets $_____ (all prices US Dollars)

Name _____ Date _____

Address _____Phone (   ) _____ – _____

City/State/Zip Code _____/_____/_____

Email _____

Card # _____ Exp Date _____
Method of Payment: (circle one) Visa/MC   American Express   Discover

VAN# _____ Billing Zip code _____ Total $_____
(last 3 numbers on back signature strip of card) (zip code where statement is sent)

Signature _____
To order call 1-(800)-615-7606 or fax completed form to 773-665-4006 or
mail with check or money order to: Bazuji Publishing LLC
3843 53rd Street SE, Tappen ND 58487 or go to ww.Bazuji.com

**I would also love to hear your comments, results, case studies, recommendations, feedback and/or anything else.
Simply put your comments below and send this in.**

Name _____   Date _____

Address _____Phone (_____) _____ – _____

City/State/Zip Code _____/_____/_____

Email _____

Fax this completed form to 773-665-4006 or Mail to: Bazuji Publishing LLC
3843 53rd Street SE, Tappen ND 58487 or go to ww.Bazuji.com